In Search of Old Shanghai

In Search of
Old Shanghai

Pan Ling

Joint Publishing (H.K.) Co., Ltd.

Published by
Joint Publishing (H.K.) Co., Ltd.
9 Queen Victoria Street, Central, Hong Kong

First published October 1982
Tenth impression April 1999

Printed in Hong Kong by
C & C Offset Printing Co., Ltd.
36 Ting Lai Road, Tai Po, N.T., Hong Kong

ISBN 962·04·0195·6

For
Leong Mo-ling
and
Ip Kung-sau

Contents

Preface

While this is not a guide-book, it may be used as a companion to one. To this end a map of Shanghai with the chief places of interest mentioned in the text is provided. The places may be located with the help of the index at the back of the book, which contains old and new street names and also their respective map references.

I should like to offer my thanks here to the people who helped me in the preparation of this book. I am indebted to Jasper Woodcock and Catherine Stenzl for their helpful reading of the manuscript; to Brian Ogden for access to the Hongkong and Shanghai Bank archives; to Louise Gibbons, Jim Hornabrook and Richard King for supplying crucial material; to Grace Lau-Ho for the printing of old photographs and to Lee Yu-wan for preparing the new ones for the press. My thanks go, above all, to my cousin Li Wei-i, whose knowledge of Shanghai straddles the old and the new, and who guided me indefatigably and superbly through both.

Pan Ling

London, 1981

1

Introduction

Much of the fascination of life in Shanghai in the decades before the 1949 Liberation lies in its strange remoteness from the world of China today. Strange that so contemporary an experience can vanish so completely — the street names changed, the capitalists fled, the glories gone, the glitter faded, the foreign residents chased out of town, the bubble burst. It was only yesterday, after all, that Shanghai was the "Paris of the East," the "capital of the tycoon," the "whore of Asia" and the "paradise of adventurers," where missionaries declared that if God let Shanghai endure He owed an apology to Sodom and Gomorrah. Its very name was unsavoury, being an English nautical slang meaning "to drug and ship as sailor when drunk." No other city fell to communism in so feverish a whirl of pleasure, dissoluteness, rapacity and squalor. Now, that image of last-fling decadence, of Shanghai dancing even while communism knocked on its door, survives only as a cliché in the minds of people, and those who witnessed it will almost certainly never see its like again.

Yet so extraordinary a past can never be entirely shaken

Shanghai skyline

off, and everywhere in Shanghai today there can be sensed the continuity of life from an earlier age. This book is an excursion to the old Shanghai, taken to be the world that tottered to its fall in 1949. It will seek the traces which remain of that world among the streets and the buildings, and in the hangovers from what is, to all intents and purposes, a bygone way of life. Physically old Shanghai may not seem hard to find at all, for sometimes it feels as if time itself is suspended in the city today, and the only changes to have occurred are the ones wrought by dereliction and decay. The city has hardly been touched by that destroyer of history's relics, the dark angel of Development, but nor has it profited much from careful preservation. The grime of years lies so thick upon its facades that it is almost as if the place is half-pickled in the deposits of history.

Yet though old Shanghai is too recently expired to have lost many of its artifacts, in some ways its relics are more elusive than those of a more ancient city, for they have not been transfixed and embalmed, like objects in a museum or epitaphs inscribed in stone, and past and present are indistinguishably mingled. In Peking the Temple of Heaven is unassailably the Temple of Heaven, delimited in space, frozen in time. It has been set apart, suitably distanced — an object of sightseeing pilgrimage, a bit of old Peking preserved. Much of old Shanghai, on the other hand, is something stumbled upon, something not immediately recognizable as a historical site or monument because it has been integrated into the present (with, as likely as not, something manifestly new tacked on to it), but with the original purpose perverted, and the old character erased.

There were three main ingredients to the flavour of old Shanghai. First, it was, by Chinese standards, a very young city, having come into the flower of its age only in the twentieth century. Here is no repository of the oldest and proudest in Chinese civilization; age is not its strong point. It saw itself in the front ranks of China's march into the modern age. Its citizens outgrew antiquated traditions quicker than any, their taste being for the very new, the very up-to-date, and the very last word in fashion. They took cultural grafts from the modern Western world in their stride, and sloughed off old customs the moment these became irreconcilable with progress. Nine out of every ten Chinese letting off firecrackers or burning incense in the Shanghai lanes, observed a famous Chinese writer in the 1930s, were Cantonese. The natives wouldn't have bothered probably, would have dismissed it all as a load of superstitious nonsense, would in any case have thought it a bad investment in future happiness, to let so much money go up in smoke for so uncertain a reward.

Secondly, Shanghai was cosmopolitan. There were really two Shanghais — the foreign and the indigenous. Early European visitors to the city often remarked that Shanghai was not Chinese; certainly it bore little resemblance to their image of China — the China of bamboo groves and willow banks, of pastoral lyrics and yearning for the past. Shanghai was indeed something unique in China. Here was the home of the "Shanghailanders," the Europeans who had made Shanghai their home. Home too of the great taipans, the merchant-adventurers, the rich compradors and the White Russian émigrés and the Jewish refugees from Nazism. Purged though it is nowadays of foreign settlers, Shanghai remains the image of what most rural Chinese conceive of as the West. To this day it is not difficult to see how closely the city conformed to the specifications of the typical British colonial outpost, with racecourse, church, waterfront, godowns and, of course, the Club.

Yet despite all that, Shanghai in its core was Chinese, but of a Chineseness that was somehow different from the rest of China. Today settlers from the provinces beyond have become so assimilated that it is often difficult to tell them apart from the native, but the term *jiangbei ren*, meaning "men from north of the (Yangzi) River" was for the Shanghainese a pejorative rather like yokel or boor. Especially wary was their attitude towards the Cantonese, those people from the far south where, as the writer Lin Yutang puts it, "beneath the Chinese culture a snake-eating aborigines tradition persists, revealing a strong admixture of the blood of the ancient Yue inhabitants of south China." Today the Shanghai native has largely forgotten that these men first came to his city as middlemen, brothel keepers and the lackeys of European opium runners, but he still turns his nose up at snake (and dog) eating, while grudgingly conceding the superiority of Cantonese cuisine as a whole.

And thirdly, without question Shanghai was one of the world's great cities. Aldous Huxley called it "Life itself. Nothing more intensely living can be imagined." In no other city, East or West, had he ever had such an impression of "dense, rank, richly clotted life." K.M. Pannikar, the Indian ambassador to China in the late 1940s, thought Shanghai an "unreal fantastic creation," the "proud Queen of the Pacific." Both at home and abroad, Shanghai has fired the imagination of novelists and film makers, and these have luridly embellished its image, and effectively projected its myths. Around the city has assembled a whole genre of literature, a corpus of film, a style of behaviour and a cast of mind. For millions of Chinese, its name was synonymous with trendiness. To this day, it has more shops bearing its name across the world than even Paris, and from Britain to Borneo, wherever a sizeable number of Chinese are gathered together, there will be found at least one hairdressing salon called "Shanghai." For it was, to the popular Chinese mind, the capital of style.

Its claim to greatness lies in much more than this, however. There was no Chinese city to equal it in hospitality to revolutionaries. All the most honoured heroes of the Chinese revolutionary saga had been sheltered here. Shanghai was the birthplace of the Chinese Communist Party, the arena of some of the fiercest political conflicts in recent history. If gangsters and gamblers were endemic to Shanghai, then so

A window recalling earlier times

were patriots, rebels and conspirators. It had witnessed scenes of great splendour and great horror. It is young of history but old of experience. And presently we shall find out if it is long of memory.

Today Shanghai is neither modern nor great; least of all is it cosmopolitan. On seeing the city again, those who knew it in its heyday are inescapably saddened. They may know with their minds that all great cities decline, that nothing in the world is permanent, yet their hearts still grieve to see the once gleaming walls blackened and blotched, the ironwork ripped out or rusted, the elegant boulevards pitted with potholes. Other eyes look back as hazily, misty with the romance of proletarian degradation and revolution. In each view nostalgia has refracted the image, and the "good old days" seem infinitely better than they were. But when each adjusts its fancies to the facts, then it is bound to see that the world of old Shanghai could not possibly have endured, and to concur with God and the missionaries that it was time it went when it did.

Huangpu River

1

Shanghai stands to the south of the Yangzi estuary at the point where the Huangpu River breaks off from the Wusong, a tributary of the Yangzi. Sidling in crook-of-the-arm fashion through the city, the Huangpu divides Shanghai into two unequal parts — the city centre and residential areas to the west, and the docks, shipyards and the industrial quarter of Pudong to the east. The Wusong, popularly known since 1916 as the Suzhou Creek, meanwhile enters the river roughly at right angles across the north. The Huangpu is at once the gut and artery of the city, the route by which Shanghai's life-stream flows, alive with every kind of traffic. Through it had chugged vessels of every description: fishing trawlers, sampans, bamboo rafts, night-soil boats, ocean liners, British, French, American and Japanese warships and cargo junks, either under massive sail or propelled by the "yuloh," the long scull peculiar to the Far East.

Shanghai is traditionally approached by boat through the Yangzi entrance and the Wusong, passing the brown sluggish mud-flats that were the humble soil from which the city sprang. The encroachment of the waters of the river upon the brown fields along the banks was once checked by dykes of stone and earth — the "bunds" to which Shanghai's famous waterfront owes its name. The boat will most likely have crossed the shallows through the North Channel, dredged some fifty years ago and almost completely dwarfing the older South Channel in river traffic. Shanghai would have been inaccessible to large ocean vessels but for the height of tide, which rises by a whole fifteen feet at the bar at spring tides. Scoured by the tides and clogging up often with the great deposits of silt brought down by the Yangzi, the Huangpu River had always depended for its life upon the breakwater and the dredger. A 1930s writer claims that you could haul up a billion cubic yards of muck and sludge a day from the river. Back in the seventeenth century, special "mud men" were employed to maintain the water routes, and it is all too easy to see why these contractors were such louts and bullies when it came to demanding pay for their labour.

Innumerable creeks once emptied themselves into the Huangpu River. Half of what is present-day Shanghai was under water until the seventh century. In a soggy landscape of shifting sand and reeds, communities of fishermen lived a life beset with uncertainty. Shanghai's origins are still discernible in its other name, Hu. This was a reference to the Hu ditches of the lower Wusong, which in turn derived their name from a fishing contraption much in use in early times. A bamboo and rope palisade driven into the river bed, this would lie flat as the tide came in and stand up again when the tide went out, trapping the fish that swam in the shallows.

Presently, over the years, the delta land and its web of waterways became a centre of waterborne trade; boats from towns along the shores of the Wusong began ranging along the China coast and beyond. In those days Shanghai was not nearly so important a port as Qinglong, a town on the Wusong. But the silting up of the Wusong clogged up

Qinglong's access to the sea and sapped its vigour. Trade began shifting to the widening Huangpu River to the south. By about the latter half of the eleventh century traffic so quickened along its banks that the place where ships were brought into dock was officially designated a town and named Shanghai, after one of the Wusong tributaries.

Gradually, administrative functions were transferred from Qinglong to Shanghai; the town was garrisoned, the first inns and schools were built. Wine storehouses, temples and monasteries, shops and dwellings sprang into life. The town was upgraded, and Shanghai became a county, a sort of town-with-hinterland division. It was not long before that time, so legend has it, that the mother of the cotton gin, one Huang Daopo, returned to her native village in Shanghai county bringing with her the sophisticated weaving and spinning techniques she had learnt from the aboriginal Li tribe in the south. Whether it was this that gave it a headstart, or the favourable natural conditions, the hinterland soon got

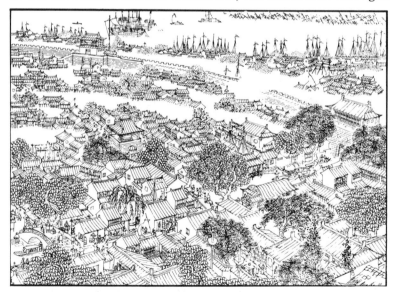

Shanghai County, 16th century

into its stride and started to grow fat on cotton. Shanghai thrived, as cloth brokers, merchants and seagoing vessels up and down the country thronged its shores.

But if the Huangpu injected commercial life into Shanghai, it also brought woe. In the mid-sixteenth century there fell upon the port successive waves of Japanese pirates. In the spring of 1553, they stormed and pillaged no less than five times in two months. That autumn the people of Shanghai felt so hard-pressed that they decided to erect a wall to keep the marauders out. The fortification was to stand for 359 years. Thus protected, Shanghai grew, steadily accumulating wealth, culture and prestige. Thickets of sail and rigging pressed against its shores. By the early years of the eighteenth century, its trade was already colossal, some 400 junks calling at its port in a week. Even before it was prised open to foreign trade by international treaty, Shanghai's trade was boasting a tonnage comparable to, or even greater than, that of London.

2

Past the muddy waters of the Huangpu ply the boats that nowadays take sightseers up and down the Shanghai river-front. Fifty years ago, they might well have rubbed shoulders with the lighters of Jardine and Matheson, or Butterfield and Swire, British firms whose names are now part of Chinese history. Certainly the passengers will have heard of Ewo, the name by which Jardine, Matheson and Company's many interests were known to the Chinese. Originally the name of William Jardine's comprador in Canton, it came to stand for cotton mills, sugar refineries, breweries, and the wharf that occupied the sweep of the harbour in front of today's Lujiadu across on the Pudong side of the river.

The name Jardine is inseparable from the story of the Opium War, the event that delivered Shanghai, once and for all, into its days of heady eminence. The passions which the war brought to the boil had been simmering for years down

A *Jardine Matheson* ship colliding with a *Butterfield & Swire* one on the Huangpu, 1896

in Canton. The Chinese did not care for the Western merchants there; "foreign devils" and "barbarians," the Cantonese called them — terms which today have lost nearly all their sting, but which must have sounded quite unfriendly then. The Europeans, for their part, found it tiresome to have to trade under the conditions laid down by the Chinese, conditions whose first aim was really to keep them out. All foreign transactions had to be conducted through the Cohong — that is, through the agency of a guild of Chinese merchants granted a monopoly by the government. Foreigners were also forbidden to remain in Canton after the trading season, so that they either had to sail home or spend the interim months in Macao. They were even denied the pleasure of boating, of excursions into the city or its environs, though three times a month they might be permitted a visit to the public gardens on an island opposite Canton, provided the trippers returned before dark and did not get drunk. Foreign women were not allowed into the "factories," the warehouses in the Canton suburb where the business was conducted, and though this pleased some hen-pecked husbands, and men with scant taste for English women, the rule did make unwilling celibates of others.

Those were the halcyon days of the opium clipper, bearing cargoes so lucrative that every foreigner in Canton save one — an American described by an observer in 1839 as a "pious, devoted servant of Christ, and a friend of China" — had a finger in the trade. The cargo was contraband, the reigning Manchu court having prohibited its importation, but this made scarcely any impression on the volume shipped in from India, and by 1837 opium accounted for well over half of all China's imports from abroad.

The British East India Company had long yielded its monopoly to private merchants, and it was this band of go-getters that was smuggling the bulk of opium into China. These men itched to push their business further inland, and chafed increasingly against the Chinese restrictions. But China was in no position to open the flood-gates. The empire was in deep crisis: for the first time in China's history, her balance of trade was overwhelmingly against her; as opium flooded in, her silver drained out.

But there was no stopping the opium runners. None strained harder at the leash than William Jardine, he whom the Chinese called Iron-headed Old Rat. He had no doubt that Chinese intransigence could be broken by a demonstration of force, and it was he who, in an interview with Lord Palmerston in London in 1838, laid before the British Foreign Secretary the blueprint for such an operation. His was the vision of history Palmerston plumped for: the despatch of a flotilla of men-of-war; the conclusion of a treaty granting free trade through Shanghai, Ningbo and other coastal ports and the occupation of islands in the Zhoushan (Chusan) archipelago and Hong Kong.

The war began with a blockade of Canton in June 1840. By July Dinghai, a town in the Zhoushan archipelago to the south of Shanghai, had fallen, an event gleefully reported by the *Times* of London: "The British flag waves over a portion of the Chinese Empire for the first time! Chusan fell into the hands of the English on Sunday, the 5th of July, and one more settlement in the Far East was added to the British Crown." On June 9, 1842, the invading force appeared within sight of the Wusong forts guarding the river approach to Shanghai itself. The British fleet under vice-admiral Sir William Parker opened fire. Under the 70-year-old Chinese commander Chen Huacheng, the fortifications along the western bank offered resistance, and his troops even made a couple of successful sorties, forcing one British ship to run aground. But the enemy forces struck chill into the hearts of the eastern garrison, and the troops there put up hardly any fight at all. So the invaders entered, sailing up-river to hoist the British flag over Shanghai, before moving on in triumph to Nanking.

This was how the periodical *Illustrated London News* described the capture of Shanghai: "The battleship *Nemesis* ... set fire to the city of Shanghai which was occupied by our troops, its public buildings burned, its rich granaries, the property of the government, given up to the people. An incessant cannonade was kept up for two hours ere the enemy showed any symptom of submission." The Treaty of Nanking and subsequent agreements with France and the United States brought peace and opened up Shanghai, along with four other places along the coast, as a "treaty port" where foreigners were permitted to trade and reside, and generally to have their way. The foreign chapter in the Shanghai story had begun.

3

When Captain George Balfour, Great Britain's first consul, got down to business in Shanghai in November 1843, there were only 23 foreign families in Shanghai. Between 1850 and 1860 they were joined by a thousand more, men working either for the consulates or for the big trading houses like Jardine and Matheson, Dent and Russell and Company. These were the first Shanghailanders, the men who stood firm upon the privileges their governments had wrested for them and looked to Shanghai for their chance of profit and glory. "In two or three years at farthest I hope to realize a fortune and get away," said one of them to his consul, "and what can it matter to me if all Shanghai disappear afterwards in fire or flood? You must not expect men in my position to condemn themselves to prolonged exile in an unhealthy climate for the benefit of posterity. We are money-making, practical men. Our business is to make money, as much and as fast as we can — and for this end all modes or means are good which the law permits."

By a series of Land Regulations concluded with the Chinese officials in Shanghai, privileged zones encircling the waterfront on the Huangpu River were established, and there the British, American and French settlers could lease land in perpetuity. The zones did not remain white enclaves for long, however, for when rebellions threatened Shanghai the Chinese flocked into them by the thousands. The Japanese came in great numbers after their victory in the 1894 Sino-Japanese war. The Chinese were not supposed to own land in these zones, but they came to do so in practice through the foreign fronts provided by Western sharks, lawyers and even missionaries, who did extremely well by these deals. The zones were to become increasingly cosmopolitan. After 1917 there was a great influx of White Russians, who filled the lower ranks of commercial life and were looked down upon by the snootier members of the European community, who thought they lowered the tone of the place. Much later waves of Jewish refugees escaping from Hitler's persecution in Europe added to the variety of nationalities, and created a "Little Vienna" in the heart of "Little Tokyo."

The British settlement was bordered to the south by a tributary of the Huangpu, the Yangjingbang or Yangjing

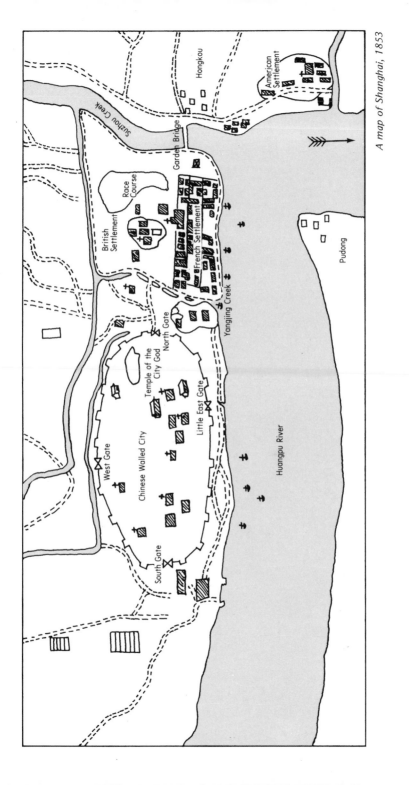

A map of Shanghai, 1853

A map of the Foreign Settlements at Shanghai, 1904

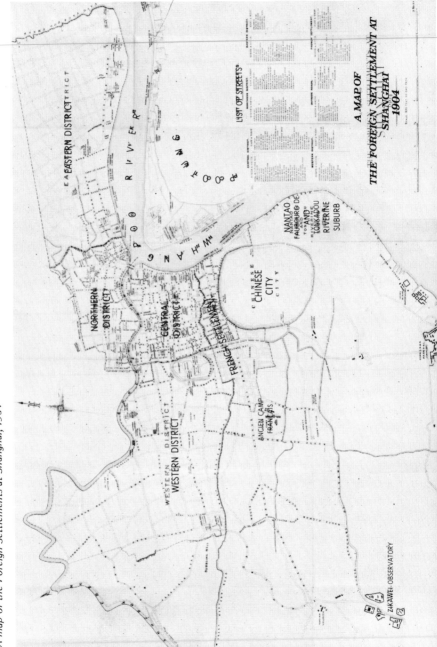

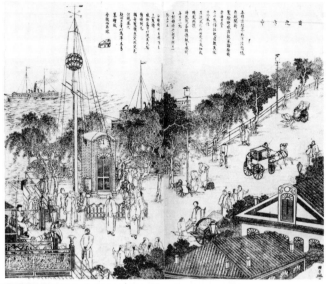

Setting up a weather vane near Yangjingbang, 1880s

Creek, and to the north by the Peking Road of later times. Today the smelly old creek is no more; Yan'an Road East now stands over it. Before it was filled in 1914, the creek was a busy thoroughfare with flotillas of barges jostling up and down its slimy waters, heavy with every kind of cargo, under sagging bridges thronged with people.

The name "Yangjingbang" has since been transmuted from a place name to a word in the Chinese vocabulary. In the early days the creek was what divided the English settlement from the French, and it was perhaps this hybrid quality which had first suggested the name to the coiner of the expression, when he groped for a word to describe Shanghai pidgin, that strangely adequate form of Anglo-Chinese communication, with its smattering of English and Portuguese terms and mock-Chinese syntax. After it was culverted the creek was turned into a boulevard and named after the English monarch Edward VII, spelt Edouard VII, naturally, on the French side.

Originally the British settlement covered no more than one square mile, but it nibbled and pushed its way ever further beyond its perimeter, until the Chinese protested, and it halted at 8.35 square miles, but allowed its roads, electricity, water mains and police authority — and with these things its influence and control — to spill over across miles of extra-settlement land. The French consul had installed himself on the other side of the Yangjingbang in a house rented from a Catholic priest, and he too expanded his domain, so that a quarter of a square mile squeezed in between the British settlement and the Chinese walled city grew to a French concession of just under four miles.

The Suzhou Creek separated the British from the American zone, established over today's Hongkou district through leases secured by the bishop W. Boone. The American and British zones merged in 1863 to form the International Settlement. The foreign community was, for all practical purposes, virtually self-governing; its members

Suzhou Creek

enjoyed the rare privilege of extraterritoriality — or "extrality" as it was called for short — and this put them beyond the reach of Chinese justice. The neutrality of the foreign zones with regard to Chinese civil wars was jealously guarded, and whenever it suited them to do so, the foreigners made their territory impenetrable to native troops, a position greatly buttressed by the warships they had moored along the Huangpu. The safety thus ensured became an incentive for the Chinese living outside to flock to the foreign settlements. By 1885, the Chinese population of the International Settlement outnumbered the foreign by nearly 35 to 1, while in the French Concession, there were some 25,000 Chinese to 300 foreigners. Western hospitality was greatly encouraged by the revenue the natives provided, for their income was taxed at a considerably higher rate than that of the foreign residents.

Chinese City

1

A ring road named Renmin (People's) Road at one end and Zhonghua (China) Road at the other encircles the network of lanes that made up the original Chinese settlement and county seat, sprawling above the crowded streets of Nanshi, the Southern Market. The ring road replaces the walls that once surrounded the quarter, erected, as it will be recalled, to ward off Japanese pirates in the mid-sixteenth century. The moat-surrounded wall was a little under three miles in length and over 27 feet in height. It was pierced by six gates oriented to the points of the compass — two to the south, two to the east, and one each to the north and west. The "water gates" let out the internal creeks to beyond the city wall. Topped by 3,600 crenelations and two watch towers, the structure was a formidable barrier, and soon put a stop to the Japanese raiders.

The gates closed after the second watch, some time before midnight, but on special occasions like weddings and funerals, arrangements could be made for one of the gates to stay open until the small hours of the morning, so as to let the guests out without too much ado. An old watchman held the keys, and as late-comers had to announce themselves to him outside the gates before they were allowed in, he came to know some of the voices very well, and could even identify the odd regular by his cough. The early Republic tore the wall down in 1912, filled in the moat, and commemorated itself by naming the roads that replaced it Zhonghua and Minguo — which joined together read "Republic of China." Aptly the French called their stretch of the ring road Boulevard des deux Républiques.

Not much of the original city has survived intact, the successive wars having reduced some parts to smoking ruins, and the corrosions of time having finished off the rest. Yet there is a feeling of unbroken continuity to the place, and it is not difficult, even now, to imagine the streets as they were. They ran according to the lane pattern typical of so much of Shanghai, in which a long, wide street branched off on both sides into many dark and narrow alleys, and ended in a

A Shanghai lane

Old and new buildings in the Chinese quarter

wooden paling that was lowered at night for safety. The alleyways were lined with low houses, and produced the characteristically Chinese vista of long, dark passages over-hung with the upright gilded signboards of open-fronted shops. Long poles, hung with washing spread out to dry, jutted out from under the eaves of dwellings, and even on San Pailou Road, the old town's main thoroughfare, it was not unusual to have one's view obstructed by dripping trousers, babies' diapers, and even women's footbinding bandages.

The impression of age was very strong, and the place was apt to be smelly. Houses huddled cheek by jowl, the shops were crammed deep with goods, the teahouses were noisy, the temples fusty and rather down-at-heel. Such domestic charms as existed were likely to be hidden from view, for the typical Chinese house looked inward; while the courtyard which stood at its core opened up to the sun and the sky, the compound was generally wrapped around with walls.

Shanghai's status as a county seat was marked by the

Chenghuang Miao, or Temple of the City God, the deity posted to keep an eye on the spirits that were abroad in Shanghai. It was descended from Jinshan Miao, or the Golden Hills Temple, built in the fifteenth century to commemorate the ancient general Huo Guang. The Temple of the City God has always been something more than a place of worship in China; it was the source of much of the colour and bustle of the city's life, the centre of its festivals and the concourse of its petty trade. Here, too, there were plum-blossom shows in the winter, orchid shows in the spring and chrysanthemum shows in the autumn, where the flowers vied against each other for awards in the "novelty," or "quality" or "rarity" category. Shanghai holds flower shows still, but they are no longer staged in the Chenghuang Miao. Nor are the other familiars — the incense and spirit-money peddlers, the story-tellers and the fortune-tellers — any more in sight, but it is still customary to go to the Chenghuang Miao on Chinese New Year's Day and to gorge oneself on the dumplings traditionally sold in the snack bars outside. The disused temple has had its ceremonial arch, stage and main hall restored to it, while all around it — almost like in the old days — cluster the teahouses, the sweet shops, the specialist shops and the throngs of Shanghai's teeming populace.

2

Nearby is the Huxinting (Heart-of-Lake Pavilion) Teahouse, a landmark mentioned in every guide to Shanghai. It stands, as its name suggests, in the middle of a lake in the Chinese city. The lake is actually more like a broad moat, once green with lotus leaves and slime. The teahouse is a pentagonal pavilion with curving roofs and painted red casements, and is approached by a wooden bridge which zigzags in nine twists across the water.

By the lake stands Yu Yuan, a classical Chinese garden created in the sixteenth century by the second son of Pan En, a high government dignitary. In its heyday the garden was

Huxinting Teahouse

very fine, but when the Pan family declined, as all great houses do, it too languished from neglect, its flowers and lacquer faded, its halls and galleries reduced to ruin. Then, in the mid-eighteenth century, a group of local gentlemen put up the money to restore the garden to its former splendour, and once more Yu Yuan became a place for rambling, with orchid shows in the spring and tea and snacks hawked along the paths throughout the year.

The landscape gardener had exact precedents to follow, and sometimes the feeling of conscious artistry hangs heavily in the air. Yu Yuan has all the ingredients of the Chinese landscape garden — labyrinthine walks, pools and rockeries, grottoes and cool retreats, feathery willows and galleries strategically sited to catch a particularly entrancing view. Some of the garden's features are very old. The Exquisite Jade Rock, a prized exhibit, is said to date from the Northern Song dynasty, when the Emperor Hui Zong, indulging his high-flown taste for curiosities, despatched his notorious rock

page 26

Ornamental rock in Yu Yuan

convoys all over the southern provinces to collect samples for his imperial park. Exquisite Jade would have been part of the imperial collection, and thus lost to Shanghai, were it not for the stormy weather on the Huangpu River, which sank the boat conveying it to the emperor. The Pan family had it hauled out of the river and erected in Yu Yuan, specially breaking a wall to move it in. It is a curious rock, porous all over like Emmental cheese, but connoisseurs point out that it satisfies all the aesthetics of rock, being *zhou, shou* and *tou* — crapy, scraggy and holey. Another aged feature is a gingko tree, which stands in a corner of the garden, ripe and doughty in its 400th year.

3

Of the pavilions in Yu Yuan, one in particular stands out: the Hall of Heralding Spring. Amidst the carved wood and gold lacquer may be found, preserved now as museum exhibits under glass, a number of relics from a bloody page in

Shanghai's history. The daggers recall the Small Swords Society, whose weapons they were. They were a Triad group led by Liu Lichuan, an ex-sugar broker or, more likely, an opium dealer from Canton, which in 1853 lay siege to the walled city and held it for nearly a year and a half. And it was in the Hall of Heralding Spring that the rebels were quartered.

Revolts launched by secret societies were a commonplace in those troubled times. From the distant mountains of Guangxi Province in southeastern China, there had risen an extraordinary upsurge, a crusade against the throne, a rebellion of the people, a movement which very nearly brought the empire to its knees. It was the Bible-armed Taipings, who had set their hearts on proclaiming a Heavenly Kingdom of Great Peace in China. Their army waged war of the most fanatical kind, their creed a ragbag of Christianity, of messianism, of secret-society brotherhood, of medieval Chinese knight-errantry. They were a ragged race, for their number was made up of the very poor — the landless peasant, the coolie, the vagrant soldier, the smuggler and the down-and-out. They cut a shaggy figure, and were sometimes called "Long Hairs," for they spurned the Manchu court's ruling that all Chinese wear a queue, and their heads looked more like mops.

Shanghai both exacerbated and benefited from the uprising. The Taiping rebels having blocked the traditional trade routes through China, the tea and silk that used to stream through Canton were now funnelled through Shanghai. While this enhanced Shanghai's commercial importance, it also ruined the porters, coolies and boatmen whose lives depended on the Canton trade. They flocked to join the Taiping movement with their knives and cudgels, having little to lose, and perhaps a kingdom to gain.

The missionaries were very keen on them at first, and thought their own efforts would now be given a tremendous boost. "The insurgents are Christian," wrote the *North China*

Herald in Shanghai, the first Western newspaper to be published in China. So great was the hope that the Taipings might, with their help, accomplish the conversion of China that the British and Foreign Bible Society printed a million copies of the New Testament in readiness. But the scene which greeted Hudson Taylor, an English missionary who arrived in Shanghai during its siege by the Small Swords Society, was not one to inspire good cheer. In a letter home in March 1854, he describes a walk around the city wall: "... sad it was to see the wreck of rows upon rows of houses near the city. Burnt down, blown down, battered to pieces — in all stages of ruin they were! And the misery of those who once inhabited them, and now at this inclement season are driven from house, home and everything, is terrible to think of." He himself had to take certain precautions, living as he did near the North Gate of the walled city, beyond the protection of the white settlements: he had a light burning all night and his "swimming belt" blown up, in case he had to dive for it at short notice after dark, when the planks of the bridge between him and the British Settlement were removed.

The fighting was fierce, with bullets and cannon balls whizzing about all day. Encamped outside the walls, the imperial forces invested the garrison and shelled it heavily. Inside the walls, provisions were brought in by cords and ladders lowered down the Northeast Gate. Liu Lichuan, the rebel commander, even had special coins minted, with the words "Taiping Coin" stamped on one side, and a sun and moon on the other. (Some of these have survived, and may be seen in the Hall of Heralding Spring.) But the Small Swords Society was doomed. The supposedly neutral French were now siding with the imperial troops, cutting the rebel's supply lines by land and sea; now famine and disease were upon them, and the rebels' defeat was in sight.

The holocaust which followed turned the city into a place of unrelieved horror. A passage from one of Hudson Taylor's letters home describes some of the atrocities: "Shanghai is now at peace, but it is like the peace of death. Two thousand people at the very least have perished ... The city is little more than a mass of ruins ... From the South to the North Gate of Shanghai on one side only, 66 heads and several bodies are exposed by sanguinary imperialists, including those of old men with white hair, besides women and children ... These terrible sights are now so common they do not upset one as they did at first."

Frederick Townsend Ward, courtesy of the Essex Institute, Salem, MA

But there were still the Taipings to ward off. To Shanghai's defence against those rebels came an American adventurer from Salem, Massachusetts, in 1860. Frederick Townsend Ward, an officer on a gunboat under British command, collected together a ragged bunch of drop-outs and beach-combers on the waterfront and, with Shanghai merchants footing the bill, turned them loose on the Taiping forces in Songjiang, just thirty miles southwest of Shanghai. But the filibusters drank far too much on the night before the attack, and Ward's high-flying adventure ended in fiasco. Still, it was his army of freebooters, backed up by a force of British, French and Chinese imperial troops, which later staved off the capture of Shanghai itself.

Both riches and honour came his way, for he had made sure that the Shanghai merchants paid him handsomely for his trouble; the Empress Dowager lionized him, and dubbed his force the Ever Victorious Army. He displayed a remark-able daring: while his men were furnished with Western artillery, he himself would never charge into battle with anything more truculent than a riding crop in his hand and a Manila cigar between his teeth. He went quite native, acquiring not only Chinese citizenship but a rich Chinese wife as well. He died when he was only thirty years old, from a mortal wound he received during an attack in 1862. He was buried with his dog in a field in Songjiang, and a Chinese temple was erected for his remains, fully endowed with altar, spirit tablet and inscription.

There was a strange sequel to his story. His considerable wealth, which he had converted into cash and negotiable securities, vanished without a trace on his death — looted, it was said, by an Englishman. This sad and quirky event seems a fit ending to his life, so nearly did it exemplify the typical Shanghai life story, with its adventure, its opportunism, its dreams of riches and glory. In spirit at least, the man from Salem was a Shanghailander through and through.

4

Waterfront

1

No change has overtaken the skyline of Shanghai's famous waterfront. A walk down Zhongshan Road East, or the Bund as it was called, is an evocation of golden days gone by. The styles of the architecture are clearly imports — the clock tower, the dome, the columns and the four-square design commemorating the British imperial presence. Even the name of the foreshore is an expression of that presence: "bund" is an Anglo-Indian word meaning embankment or quay, and bespeaks old Shanghai's connections to the sweep of the British Empire.

The first glimpse of the waterfront was often a surprise to the European visitor, for it looked so un-Chinese, and so curiously like home. Catching sight of it on board his ship in 1886, Maurice Jametel, a French sinologist, was struck at once by the European villas along its length, with their smart white facades and elegant balconies, and the rows of trees in front. An array of magnificent buildings surveyed the quay, and with their neat lawns and well-kept flower beds, they called to mind a plush suburb in Paris.

View of the Bund

The port was already a hive of activity, with British and German launches flurrying along the river, and loading cranes whirring into place. There was a flash of galvanized iron from the roofs of the godowns behind the mansions. And as the boat chugged further upstream, the styles of the buildings came into focus, and they looked, to our French sinologist's eye, "more wealthy than elegant," "bizarre rather than beautiful." There were the city's leading banks — the Hongkong and Shanghai Bank, the Oriental Bank, the Agra Bank, the Mercantile and the Chartered Bank and the Comptoir d'Escompte de Paris — massed along the quay in veritable palaces.

The Bund proper began at Garden Bridge (today's Waibaidu Bridge) to the north, and stretched for about half a mile to Rue du Consulat (today's Jinling Road East) in the south. The Bund was part promenade, part thoroughfare and part business hub. There was no better way to advertise the worth and standing of your business than to site its office there, to have its burnished brass insignia on one of its doors. Then you'd be among the grandest and the best: the Glen Line, Asiatic Petroleum Company, David Sassoon and Sons. There the tall clock tower of the Customs House jutted, here the Shanghai Club beckoned. A multitude of flagpoles, each unfurling a national flag, pushed out of the masonry as though jostling for air. There were probably more flag posts per capita in Shanghai, thought an American resident in the 1920s, than in any other city in the world, and you would think, coming up the Huangpu for the first time, that some holiday was being celebrated, so like a gala did it look.

2

Linking the American enclave to the British, Garden Bridge was the first of a series of twelve bridges that would presently span the Suzhou Creek. The Chinese called it *Waibaidu Qiao* or the Bridge of the Outer Ferry, for, standing as it did at the point where the creek waters spilled into the

View of the former American Settlement and Russian Consulate from Waibaidu Bridge

Waibaidu Bridge

Huangpu, it marked what used to be the outermost terminus of the ferry crossings. It started life as a wooden structure, built in 1856 by an Englishman named Wills. As a toll was exacted for crossing it, Mr Wills was soon a very rich man.

The Chinese users paid cash, but the Europeans generally crossed it on credit. This caused much bad feeling between the races, and the Chinese decided to keep away and fall back on their own ferryboats instead. In the end the Municipal Council stepped in, built another bridge a dozen paces from Mr Wills's, and allowed everyone to traverse it for free. Mr Wills was bought out and his bridge dismantled. The Chinese continued to call its replacement Waibaidu Qiao; only now, by a play upon one of the three Chinese characters that made up that name, the meaning was altered to the Bridge of Free Outer Crossing.

The structure was completely revamped in 1906, steel girders taking the place of timber. As it was 60 feet wide and divided into two spans, each of 171 feet, every form of conveyance could be found crossing it. Down it darted the rickshaw, first introduced to Shanghai from Japan by a Frenchman; up it clanged the tram, a British contribution. The motorcar appeared in 1901, imported by a Hungarian, the pedicab in 1926, produced much nearer home. The two-wheeled coster's barrow bumped across it, as recognizably indigenous as the coolie who, like some draught animal, pushed it and pulled it along.

After the outbreak of the Sino-Japanese War in 1937 the bridge separated the Japanese-occupied areas to the north of Suzhou Creek (Zhabei and Hongkou) from the International Settlement. Guarded at one end by Japanese sentries and at the other by British ones, the bridge was a sort of no man's land, all sandbags and barbed wire. Chinese pedestrians crossing it had to doff their hats and bow to the Japanese guards, and if they did not do so deferentially enough, were often prodded with bayonet or slapped in the face. A Reuters despatch from Shanghai on March 30, 1938 reported an incident in which Japanese soldiers set upon an old Chinese man on the bridge, beat him up, and threw him into the creek. The British soldiers posted at the other end were helpless, and watched the old man drown to the sound of Japanese cheering and laughter.

But in their way the Chinese sometimes got their own back. Trams crossing the bridge had to pull up at the top and ask for permission to cross. The driver had to make this request in Japanese and quite often, he would twist his syllables so that the sentence came out in a Shanghainese obscenity enjoining the Japanese sentry to do something dire to his mother. What the Chinese passengers and passers-by relished most of all was when the Japanese sentry unwittingly shouted his agreement, thinking he was only giving leave to pass.

3

Today's Huangpu Park, close by Waibaidu Bridge, was once the Public Gardens, the pride and joy of the British community, but the symbol of monstrous humiliation to the Chinese. For many years it was closed to the ordinary native, for there was a sign on the gate forbidding his entry. It did not exactly read, as all Shanghainese now like to claim, "Dogs and Chinese Not Allowed." Still, among the list of regulations prominently displayed on the board, one stipulated the inadmissibility of dogs, and another the exclusion of the Chinese. An exception was made in the case of native servants accompanying their white employers, but this was obviously to provide for the Chinese nannies bringing their foreign charges into the park. What particularly irked the Chinese was the fact that the garden was paid for out of municipal taxes levied on Chinese and Europeans alike, and stood on an acre of reclaimed foreshore filled in with Chinese soil.

The British, for their part, were intensely proprietorial towards it. To them it was a fragment of England, and the

Entrance to Huangpu Park

natives would only spoil it. The park had been created by a
Scottish gardener brought out specially for this purpose, and
they were determined to keep the green lawns and the rose
bushes, the herbaceous borders and hedges, the iron pavilion
and its music stands all to themselves. The Chinese taxpayers
were furious, and complained to the Municipal Council,
which in the end relaxed the rules, but only to admit
"well-dressed" Chinese issued with warrants to enter. The
point was, of course, that this was no place for the hoi polloi.
Just to drive it home a sentinel was posted at the gate and —
to the Chinese this was the worst insult of all — the man was
a Sikh, that familiar figure of old Shanghai, complete with
turban, beard and truncheon. To the Shanghainese the Sikh
policeman, whom they called that Red-Headed So and So
behind his back, was an object of fear and loathing. They
bitterly resented his servile attitude towards the British, who
had brought him out to Shanghai, perhaps failing to realize
that, like them, the Sikh would probably give anything to

cock a snook at the British.

Across the road from the Huangpu Park is the Friendship Store. This is housed in what used to be the British Consulate, which once stood solidly in the middle of a velvety English lawn, on a site acquired by the first British Consul, Sir Rutherford Alcock, in 1848. The first consulate had burned down in 1870, and had had to be completely rebuilt. Down the Bund to the south three other buildings powerfully recall the British presence: the Customs House clock tower; the Hongkong and Shanghai Banking Corporation, now the seat of the People's Municipal Government, the city's Party Revolutionary Committee and the Committee for Military Control of the People's Liberation Army; and right down at the end, the Shanghai Club, now the Dongfeng Hotel.

Presiding over the bustle of the Huangpu quayside, the Customs House was erected in 1927 to replace its predecessor, a Tudor-style building which looked as though it had been lifted straight out of England. The statue of an Irishman, Sir Robert Hart, once stood in front of it. During the war the Japanese removed it, and now only his work — in hydrology, conservancy, harbour regulations, navigational aids and the adoption of standard time by China — survives him in Shanghai. Robert Hart was the notoriously autocratic Inspector General of the Imperial Chinese Customs Service and the most powerful Westerner in China at the close of the nineteenth century. The foreign-staffed customs service started off as a stopgap, a temporary arrangement created by Rutherford Alcock for delegates of the Western treaty powers to superintend the collection of customs duties while Shanghai lay in the grip of the Small Swords Society. The Chinese official who agreed to this was Wu Jianzhang, a merchant from Canton whose success in wangling the prefectship of Shanghai had redounded most profitably to his business with the foreigners. The outbreak of the rebellion had sent him scurrying for refuge to the foreign enclave,

Rutherford Alcock

which had been declared neutral by the treaty powers and was safe from the hostilities. After these subsided he returned to the Chinese fold only to hand over the collection of custom imposts on foreign trade to the Western consuls.

The customs service eventually became an imperial affair and its headquarters was transferred from Shanghai to Peking. The first inspector-general had been Horatio Nelson Lay, an Englishman with a dazzling command of the Chinese language, but few friends among the Chinese themselves. However it was his successor, Robert Hart, who made it the stupendous thing that it was.

Next to the Customs House, the Hongkong and Shanghai Banking Corporation. When it was built in 1921, replacing the older, scarcely less handsome building, it took two years, one month and ten days. It was a hefty pile of granite, with a splendid dome on top and a pair of crouching bronze lions at the door. It was the finest building, so people thought, to be found anywhere between Suez and the Bering Straits. The

Hongkong and Shanghai Bank on the occasion of its opening

Attending the opening of the Hongkong and Shanghai Bank

lions have long since disappeared, which is perhaps just as well, since they are hardly emblematic of revolutionary committees and people's government. It was assumed that they were removed and melted down for cannon by the Japanese during the war, but one Chinese account says that the lions actually survived the Japanese and were discovered, one day in 1946, hidden away in a workroom in the bank. No one is altogether sure of their whereabouts today.

No. 3 The Bund (now No. 3 Zhongshan Road East I) was once the Shanghai Club, a transplant on Chinese soil of the snobbish traditions of the London club, with its suggestion of gin and whisky, snoozes after tiffin, and natives-and-riffraff-not-allowed. The premises were handsome, the furnishings plush, the marble hall smacked of money, the famous Long Bar of *camaraderie* among The Boys. The regulars were toffs, and the Club was the stronghold of their dignity. It lay at the heart of British expatriate life in Shanghai, in much the same way as clubs did throughout the British Empire — a life characterized by rich food, excessive drinking, balls and *soirées* and an abundance of servants. Here, course by course, is the menu of the Shanghai expatriate's dinner in the early days of the treaty port: "rich soup, and a glass of sherry; *then* one or two side dishes with champagne; *then* some beef, mutton, or fowls and bacon, with *more* champagne, or beer; *then* rice and curry and ham; *afterwards* game; *then* pudding, pastry, jelly, custard, or blancmange, and *more* champagne; *then* cheese and salad, and bread and butter, and a glass of port wine; *then* in many cases, oranges, figs, raisins, and walnuts ... *with* two or three glasses of claret or some other wine." It is not impossible, if you exercise your imagination a little, to feel this sumptuousness still, as you wander through the rooms of the Dongfeng Hotel.

4

The Peace Hotel, which stands at the corner of Nanking Road East and the waterfront, has two wings, one on the north side of Nanking Road and one on the south. The latter was formerly the Palace Hotel; the former was the Sassoon House, part of which accommodated the Cathay Hotel, at one time the pearl of Shanghai hostelry. Once parties of legendary splendour were held in its ballroom and rooftop restaurant, and almost all the world came to stay. Noel Coward did in the winter of 1930, and it was while nursing his influenza in one of its rooms that he completed the draft of his famous play *Private Lives.*

He has left us with a glimpse of the social whirl of the hotel set. In his memoirs *Present Indicative* he writes: "There were lots of parties and Chinese dinners and cosmopolitan junketings which, while putting a slight strain on our lingual abilities, in no way dampened our spirits. We found some charming new friends, notably Madame Birt and her twin daughters who, apart from being extremely attractive, could quarrel with each other in six different languages without even realizing that they were not sticking to one; and three English naval officers ... with whom we visited many of the lower and gayer haunts of the city ...."

Shanghai did indeed shelter a medley of races, becoming so cosmopolitan in the early 1940s that the large hotels found it necessary to advertise their ability to speak to their patrons, as a minimum, in English, French, German and Russian. And if one looked across the Huangpu River from the top of the Cathay Hotel, one would find this cosmopolitanism reflected in the harbour, where a fleet of American, British, French and Italian warships rode at anchor.

One may remember that this cosmopolitanism was bred of battle, and that what brought the nations of the world to this harbour in the first place were the unbelievable prizes to be won from opium. It was on such prizes that the Sassoon dynasty was built. The Cathay Hotel, completed in 1930, was the creation of Ellice Victor Sassoon, the grandson of Elias Sassoon, founder of the company E.D. Sassoon. Elias was the second son of the patriarch of the clan, David Sassoon, a

Jewish merchant from Baghdad. The family had emigrated to Bombay to avoid persecution in Baghdad, and there it had thrived on the rich trade in cotton and opium. Elias Sassoon first came to China in 1844, and it struck him at once that nowhere were the prospects for the two commodities brighter than in Shanghai and Hong Kong. Soon the family firm David Sassoon and Sons was ensconced in Shanghai, trading furiously and piling up enormous profits. When the father died, the two eldest brothers split up, Elias resigning from the family firm to found his own company, E.D. Sassoon. In Shanghai the two great houses came to be distinguished as the Old and New Sassoon. Silas Hardoon, another Jew from Baghdad whose name would pass into Shanghai legend, was to work for both, before leaving to make a colossal fortune on his own.

The elder Sassoon had become naturalized as a British subject in India, and as the Sassoon fortune grew and the family proliferated, the gay life of London's high society beckoned to him with increasing allure. Some branches of the Sassoon family decided to settle in England and there, in lordly houses in town and country, the Sassoon cousins achieved eminence, knighthoods, marriage to the Rothschilds and ever greater magnificence. Meanwhile their business interests ramified throughout the Far East, their name so compelling in India and Shanghai that when Sir Albert, Elias's elder brother, died in London in 1896, scores of Jewish and Parsee shops closed for the day in India and the flags flew at half-mast on all the opium ships on the Huangpu River.

In Shanghai the house of Sassoon was raised to its height of power and success by Ellice Victor Sassoon, nicknamed Eve from his initials EV during his student days at Trinity College, Cambridge, where he took a mediocre degree in History. Once in charge of the operations at E.D. Sassoon, he pushed his empire up through the streets of the Settlement, snapping up a luxury apartment block here, taking over hotels and properties there. From the third floor of Sassoon House, he grandly dominated the real estate market in Shanghai.

But he saw it all go sour. His era spanned a changing China, a China convulsed by war and revolution. A bomb wrecked the entrance of the Cathay Hotel; Japanese soldiers stripped his luxury apartments of radiators for scrap; he saw Shanghai flooded by waves of refugees. He saw the glitter fading, but when it all ended, in the spring of 1949, he showed no outward pang, knowing that most of his Shanghai assets were safe in the Bahamas. "Well, there it is," he said, when the news of the communist takeover came to him in New York, "I gave up India and China gave me up."

Yet he had had a good run for his money. As he had worked, so had he lived — with panache. Shanghai had allowed him to give full play to his talent for pleasure, his passion for the turf, his hearty sexual appetite, his taste for expensive ivories and jade. In India he drove a huge yellow car with the number plate EVE 1; in Shanghai his parties were legendary. He was nattily dressed, and liked to be seen everywhere with a fashionable lady on his arm. He loved horses, and kept over a hundred of them, maintaining always that "there is only one race greater than the Jews, and that's the Derby."

But sometimes his enjoyment of life was dulled by physical discomfort and self-consciousness. He had been crippled by a flying accident in the First World War, and was convinced that no one would marry him except for his money. He did marry in the end (an American nurse who looked after him in his final years), but not until he was 78. Throughout his later life he was never entirely free from pain, and wherever he went his two walking sticks would go with him. For all that he was a star turn in Shanghai's dance of death. Like so many of his contemporaries, he had to pack his bags and pay his bills once the Chinese took over. But he had made his mark on the city, and though it no longer

Sassoon House

carries his name, Sassoon House remains a lasting memorial. His mansion at 2409 Hongqiao Road, next door to the Shanghai Zoo, is another relic. Gable-roofed and timber-framed, the building was meant to have the air of a hunting lodge, and stood among handsome groves of maple and poplar. Victor Sassoon sold the property to a flamboyant Ningbo tycoon called James Lee shortly before the Japanese overran Shanghai. Since then the building has been a Japanese naval headquarters, a gambling casino, the private villa of the Gang of Four, and the rented office and residence of the British Petroleum Company.

5

Money was Shanghai's *raison d'être*, and the Bank of China, standing next door to Sassoon House, was its stronghold. This building will always be associated with the chaos wreaked by the Kuomintang government on Chinese

Bank of China

currency in the years immediately before its fall, when the rate of inflation ran amok and Shanghai's citizens had to go shopping with sacks of worthless money. Above all, the bank was inextricably linked to the wheeling dealing of T.V. Soong, Madame Chiang Kai-shek's brother, and Dr H.H. Kung, his brother-in-law. (In anglicising their names by placing the initials of the first name before the family name, Soong and Kung were following a practice fashionable in Shanghai at the time.)

Born in Shanghai, T.V. Soong studied at the St John's College there and then went to Harvard. His distinctly Yankee style posed a sharp contrast to his brother-in-law, who wore Chinese silk robes and affected the manner of the old-school Chinese gentleman. Between them they controlled the four largest banks — the Bank of China, the Central Bank, the Communications Bank and the Farmers Bank — and turned them into the instrument of their own enrichment and power. In their dealings the lines between public and private were always blurred, they and the rest of that extraordinary family elevating the practice and enjoyment of nepotism to the level of art.

Few families are as fascinating. Here was Charlie Soong, a Methodist Episcopal pastor indoctrinated in North Carolina, settling down in Shanghai — but never in all his life to Chinese food. Here was his eldest daughter Eling (Madame H.H. Kung), scandalizing Shanghai by her shady commodity and currency speculation; here was his youngest daughter Mayling (Madame Chiang Kai-shek), a sworn enemy of communism, and there was her sister Ching Ling (Madame Sun Yat-sen), as Red as Red could be. Like the English Mitfords, there is the paradox of political sympathies as widely divergent as fascism and communism combining in a single family.

During the last war when the rate of exchange between the Chinese and US. dollar was pegged at twenty to one, the Kungs and T.V. Soong coolly bought American dollars at the declared rate and sold them on the black market at ten times the official value. The Chiangs siphoned off huge amounts of American funding and had them stashed away in bank accounts in the United States. When inflation soared the Chiang government issued bank notes of colossal denominations, itself assuming control of the gold, silver and US dollars in China. The price index leapt from 100 in 1937 to 627,210 by the end of 1947. When the government esta-

Soong Mayling

blished the gold yuan as the new currency unit at a fixed rate of four gold yuan to US$1, businessmen who did not comply with the exchange regulations were publicly executed in Shanghai. But inflation came bouncing back nonetheless, and went so beserk that workers would rather be paid by their factories in goods than in money. All over Shanghai pavements, stalls were hurriedly rigged up to sell off such goods, and the moment the money had changed hands, it would be rushed off to the nearest rice shop, to be plunked down at the till before the price had had time to go up again. Among the poor this bred chronic insecurity on an unimaginable scale.

Nanking Road

1

Sprawling behind the waterfront is the mosaic of Shanghai's streets and lanes. There was a time when the street names read like a roster of the other outposts of the British Empire — Benares Road, Kabul Road, Sandakan Road, Simla Road and so on. But the names never did catch on, and they eventually gave way to those suggested by places in the Chinese hinterland. Many others have had at least one change of name — from an older, European one evoking dignitaries from distant lands to a newer, Chinese replacement that puts one more in mind of home. There were streets commemorating Rutherford Alcock, the British consul; Sir Robert Hart, of Chinese Maritime Customs fame; Sir Walter Medhurst, the sinologue and consul, and other British men who had left their mark on Shanghai. But they in their turn became anachronisms, and names less offensively exotic took their place — Anguo (Nation at Peace) for Alcock; Changde (Perpetual Virtue) for Hart, and Taixing (Surpassing Prosperity) for Medhurst. Nor were the American eponyms spared. Take Tanggu Road, which has supplanted the name of the missionary whose quest for cheap land on which to build his church had led to the United States digging her heels in at Hongkou. It used to be called Boone, or "Boong" as the Shanghainese trolleybus conductors had it, as they bellowed it out at its approach. But to this day past and present are sometimes blurred, the citizens clinging to the original English names — or rather the Chinese transliterations of them — long after they had been changed.

Immediately behind the northern stretch of the waterfront the streets cross each other in a grid, almost at right angles, those running from north to south taking the names of China's provinces, and those running east to west the names of her cities. In the vernacular some of these streets were numerically named, so that Nanking Road was customarily referred to as the First, Jiujiang Road just below it as the Second, Hankou Road as the Third and Fuzhou Road as the Fourth.

In this knot of streets the ways of the traditional market town were vigorously alive still, with the craftsmen and traders in the same line of business congregating along a single street. There was hardly a soul in Shanghai who did not know that the middle stretch of Fuzhou Road was "culture street," where the great booksellers like Zhonghua, World and Great East were to be found, and where the scholar or collector could indulge his appetite for anything from translations of European classics to the Chinese comic. He could rummage about in the studios, as the arty bookshops were called, or in the tiny stationery shops and, depending entirely upon his fancy, stock himself up with writing brushes or Parker pens, ink sticks or bottles of Quink, vermilion seal pads or rubber chops.

Everybody knew that for secondhand clothes you went to Fujian Road, for ladies' shoes to Zhejiang Road; that the herbalists were to be found in Fuzhou Road, the best cut in men's suits in Avenue Joffre (today's Huaihai Road). Such was the degree of specialization that while you bought rice

A view of Shanghai

View of customshouse clock tower from the Huangpu

Huangpu river boats

Ningbo dumpling shop near Chenghuang Miao

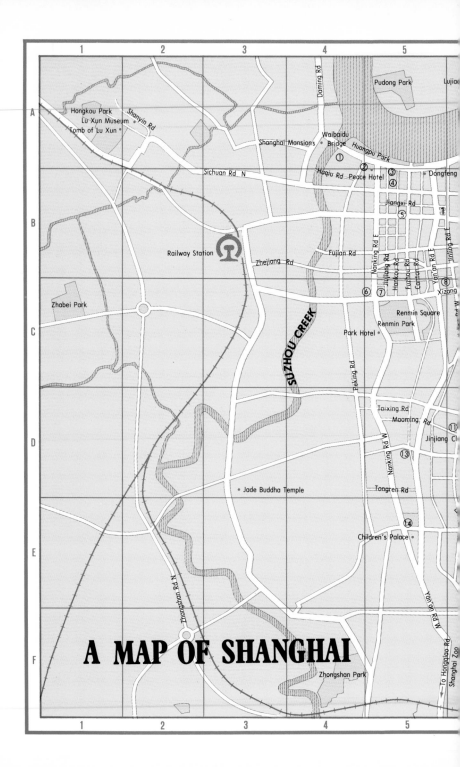

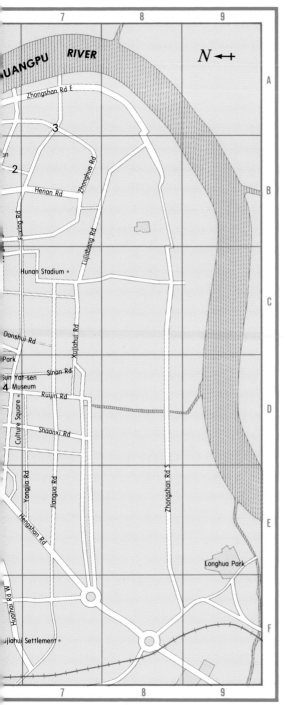

LEGEND

1. Friendship Store
2. Bank of China
3. Customs House
4. People's Municipal Government
5. Municipal Council
6. No. 1 Department Store
7. Peiguang Middle School
8. Youth Palace
9. Taoyuan Estate
10. CCP First National Congress Venue
11. Shanghai Art Theatre
12. Roman Catholic Cathedral
13. Industrial Exhibition Hall
14. Jing'an Shrine

1 Xikou Rd
2 San Pailou Rd
3 Little East Gate
4 Xiangshan Rd

Tomb of Lu Xun

Sassoon villa and part of grounds

Sassoon villa at Hongqiao Road

Peace Hotel

down at Shiliupu, in the Chinese bit of the waterfront, you bought eggs at Tiantong Road; while you bought dried seafood on Minguo Road, you bought fresh fish in the market near Little East Gate. There was a street which sold nothing but pink baby bonnets, and a section of the Canton Road that had enough theatre costumes and props to fill all the stages of Shanghai.

Every Shanghainese could tell you where the red light district was. In the Fuzhou Road teahouse and bordello, the Chinese institution of the singsong girl (a hostess, a geisha, an escort, an artiste, mere decoration at parties, a whore) was perfected. That these ladies usually hailed from Suzhou was

*Two singsong girls fighting over
a client on Fuzhou Road, 1895*

probably due not so much, as is widely believed, to the fact that the women there are the loveliest, as to the singular effect which their speech has upon the ear: while the Suzhou lilt sounds absurdly coy coming from men, from the lips of women it can melt the heart of almost any man. Today there is nothing left of the world of the singsong girl, but this is not only because it is incompatible with the prevailing political ethos. Even if the new government had not swept it all away, the institution would have withered (ordinary prostitution replacing it), as the relationships of Chinese couples change and women grow less amenable with increasing economic independence. In the days of arranged matches, romantic love or affinity was hardly ever a consideration in marriage, and so the husband had to look elsewhere for his pleasure, for companionship, and for all those wifely attentions which these professional women could give with such abundance, and often with such style.

Nanking Road is the busiest and longest of them all. It intersects twenty-six streets, to end in the spring that gave the western section of the thoroughfare its English name — Bubbling Well Road. Jing'an Road, the former Chinese name, is still sometimes preferred to Nanking Road West by some of Shanghai's citizens, although the shrine from which the name derived, the Jing'an or Tranquillity Shrine, housed a plastics factory until its recent restoration.

Nanking Road testifies to the love of horses embedded deeply in the bones of the Englishman, for its progressive extension from the old Garden Lane, a short strip linking the waterfront to the city's very first racecourse on today's Henan Road, was prompted by the search for new courses and bridle paths. When property prices shot up around the old Garden Lane, the shareholders of the Shanghai Racing Course were quick to place their prize slab of real estate on the market. Property further afield was acquired; a new swath was cut. This swept implacably through field and homestead, graveyard and coffin, heedless of the Chinese

Jing'an Shrine

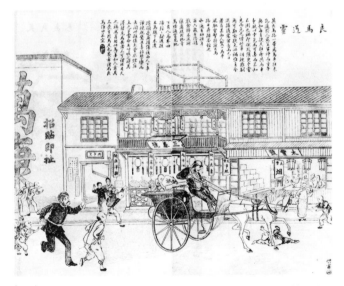

Foreigner's horse trampling on Chinese pedestrian on Nanking Road, 1895

reverence for the dead, and defying a certain Li Xianyun, a would-be Small Swords Society rebel, who protested with hoe and stick, and called for death to the foreign devils. With the completion of this extension, Garden Lane became formally known as Nanking Road. Yet another plot was acquired in 1862, and it was here that the third and best known of the Shanghai racecourses was built, with the tree-lined Bubbling Well Road, as this last section was called, edging in towards it in a wide and graceful curve.

Today there is almost no trace of the world of "the turf" left. Gone are the punters, the bookmakers, the Cup Races, the well-trained thoroughbred horses and the well-dressed thoroughbred socialites, the trainers and the scalpers, who bought up blocks of seats for their regular clients. The Club buildings are now the Shanghai Municipal Library, and only the grandstand in front (nowadays serving as a rostrum for meetings) retains any suggestion of the past. Half the old racecourse is now Renmin (People's) Park, a splodge of

Back from the races, early 1940s

Shanghai Library

Renmin Square

welcome green, and half is Renmin Square, a slab of dusty concrete.

The Shanghainese were inordinately proud of Nanking Road, not only because of its shops overflowing with goods, but because there was truly nothing like it in the rest of China. It was so modern, and nothing enthralled the Shanghainese more than modernity. While the rest of the nation was still sunk in rusticity, here were young girls clacking about on Italian heels, photographic studios, department stores, special offers and seasonal sales, and publicity gimmicks which called for bands to play and even a dwarf got up in a top-hat to cry "Fantastic value! Fantastic value!" outside the shop.

The atmosphere was dictated by the presence of the Big Four — the Wing On (now the Number Ten Department Store), Sincere (currently the Shanghai Clothing Store), Sun Sun (now the Number One Provisions Store) and The Sun (today's Number One Department Store). In their heyday

Number Ten Department Store

Number One Provisions Store

these department stores were more than a collection of shop counters: people came here not only to snap up bargains, but to take tea and cold refreshment, to dine and dance, to listen to oratorios and Shaoxing opera, to skate, to watch comic performances, to look at exhibitions of painting and calligraphy, to play ping-pong and billiards, and to cool down with a pink ice-cream or two.

It was in this most bustling of thoroughfares that, at one o'clock on an August afternoon, 47 days after the outbreak of the 1937 Sino-Japanese war, a bomb fell and exploded. It landed square on the third-floor balcony of Sincere, plunging the building into a haze of shattering glass and gushing water. A double-decker bus in the street below swerved and crashed, and terror gripped the milling crowds. When the panic subsided, 600 were found wounded, and a hundred lay dead, including a Sikh policeman caught in the middle of directing traffic at the junction with Zhejiang Road. (For though a contemporary English guidebook to China claims for Shanghai the distinction of being the first city in the world to regulate traffic by light signals, those turbaned figures on their round platforms were still a familiar sight at main intersections.)

Chinese authorities hastily branded it an act of enemy aggression, and it was put about that the Japanese had meant it for high-ranking Chinese officers who, so Japanese intelligence had wrongly supposed, were gathered in Sincere's Dongya Restaurant that afternoon. There was also the rumour that it was dropped by the Chinese airforce itself, for it had made similar gaffs before (earlier that month, two bombs had been dropped by mistake at the place where Nanking Road met the Bund, and no one would put it past the Chinese pilots to do it again).

2

Two other sites in the vicinity of Nanking Road have been rich in incident. Go round the corner into Guizhou Road, and you will find the building which once housed the infamous Laozha Police Station. Now the Peiguang Middle School, the police station was a "bold and well-proportioned building" where, so a 1920s guide tells us, "permission to see the prisoners in their iron exercise cages may usually be granted." The place is no longer a chamber of horrors, but it should stimulate your historical sense all the same, for around it was enacted one of the climacteric scenes in Chinese annals.

This was the May Thirtieth killing in 1925, an incident which historians say marked the beginning of the finale of Western imperial power in China. What triggered it all off was the killing of a Chinese worker in the Japanese-owned Naigai Wata Mills in a clash between the workers and the management. At about noon on May 30, an alert went out to all the police stations that crowds were gathering around an anti-Japanese demonstration, and that things just might get out of hand. However, the semi-annual race meeting of the Club on Bubbling Well Road was on and Kenneth McEuan, the

Peiguang Middle School, formerly Laozha Police Station

commissioner of the Shanghai Municipal Police, thought that he would slip out for a drink and a spot of tiffin at the Shanghai Club before proceeding to an agreeable afternoon at the races. It was left to Inspector Everson, the man in charge of the Laozha station, to deal with the commotion by himself. He arrested 23 students altogether, but hundreds more appeared outside the station, demanding the release of those who had been locked up there. Presently the numbers swelled to some 1,500 to 2,000, many breaking into the station itself. The agitation reached such a pitch that Everson began to feel menaced. So he shouted a warning that if it did not calm down, he would shoot. Ten seconds later, he gave the order to fire; no sooner had he done this than 44 shots rang out. In a matter of moments it was all over, the crowd dispersed in fear and confusion, and the street a litter of bodies — some dead, many wounded, and all hideously bespattered with blood.

The event is deeply engraved in the Chinese memory, for afterwards not only did 150,000 workers in Shanghai go on strike in protest, but the shore parties of as many as 26 gunboats were landed by the International Settlement, and no less than ten other cities in China also downed tools in sympathy. In Shanghai 50,000 students walked out of their classes and shops closed their doors. The foreign press thought it all a Bolshevik plot, but the more percipient of the foreign observers saw the groundswell for what it was, and in the distance heard the knell — faintly yet, but growing louder by the hour.

The other site is located at the corner of Fuzhou and Henan Road. There you will find a massive building currently housing, among other municipal offices, the city's health bureau, environment department, labour department and the Shanghai Red Cross. The building was once the headquarters of the International Settlement's Municipal Council. The citadel of Western, and particularly British, power in Shanghai, the Council engaged in public works, levied taxes,

*Former Municipal Council head-
quarters*

Former Municipal Council headquarters

policed the streets and generally ran the settlement. One of
its departments was the Volunteer Corps, a foreign
townsmen's militia called to action whenever the rumbles of
one of those popular movements that punctuated Chinese
history were felt in Shanghai. For though the white man
lorded it over the Chinese, still, as the popular saying went:
"The people are afraid of the mandarins, the mandarins are
afraid of the foreign devils, but the foreign devils are afraid
of the people." However, the people, though they formed the
bulk of the settlement's population, had no representation in
municipal government until quite late in the day. The
French, ever ones for going it alone (or at least, for going
without the English), had their own Conseil d'Administration
Municipal, their own electric light works, tramway system
and gendarmerie.

Another curious institution was the Mixed Court, which
tried civil and criminal cases involving Chinese residents in
the International Settlement. The original intention was for a
Chinese magistrate to try these cases, assisted by a foreign

assessor, usually the consul or his deputy. How it worked out in practice was that whenever a difference of opinion arose between the two ends of the bench, the Chinese opinion invariably turned out to be the minority one. It was soon decided that Chinese judgement could never stand up to the scrutiny of the British mind, with its sense of justice and fair play, and it were as well if the assessor took over as judge — never mind that he had no legal training to speak of.

Many stories are embedded in the court records. One, a 1905 *cause célèbre*, tells of a Mrs Li, a Cantonese matron hauled before the magistrate, accompanied by fifteen girls and more than a hundred pieces of luggage. She was charged with kidnapping the young ladies for immoral purposes. The evidence failed to satisfy the Chinese magistrate, and he decided at the end of the hearing that she should be remanded in court custody. The British assessor thought she should go to gaol. A few sharp words were exchanged between the two sides of the bench and, brooking no damned impertinence from the native, the assessor (who happened to be the British vice-consul) ordered the Municipal Police to take Mrs Li away. A scuffle broke out in the courtroom when some Chinese attendants tried to stop this, but the Municipal Police fought them off and willy-nilly, bundled the protesting lady out of the room and into the Municipal lock-up.

Local loyalties, ever strong in China, were stirred up in the Cantonese Guild in Shanghai. The members took up Mrs Li's cause and instituted inquiries. From the replies, it would appear that, far from being the procuress she was thought to be, the lady was the respectable widow of a Sichuanese official who at that very moment was lying in his coffin among the hundred pieces of luggage. The young girls were merely domestics accompanying the lady to Sichuan, where she was to bury her husband. The Guild members were outraged, and lodged protests at once. Consular telegrams darted between Shanghai and Peking until, on the sixth day of her incarceration, Mrs Li was released, her gaolers depositing her, not into the custody of the court, as would perhaps have been proper, but unceremoniously on the doorstep of the Cantonese Guild hall.

The Chinese were galled by the whole affair and, closing all their shops one morning, they swept up Nanking Road to stage a demonstration outside Laozha Police Station. Upon this grim building one crowd launched its attack; down the

Demonstration outside Laozha Police Station, 1905

road, another assailed the Town Hall. At some stage in the proceedings the police station was set ablaze, the crowds fired upon by policemen, and the demonstration thrown into utter disarray. By noon the foreign residents had summoned the Volunteers Corps, and arranged for a naval landing party to be put ashore. British might prevailed, as it nearly always did in those days, and within hours it was business as usual. The local citizens did not gain much by their self-assertion: though nearly a dozen Chinese lives were lost, for their part the British considered honour quite properly served by their agreement to transfer the browbeating vice-consul to another town.

3

Xizang, or Tibet, Road divides Nanking Road into its eastern and western stretches. In the first two decades of the century, you crossed Tibet Road westwards to enter upon what was much the poshest part of town in which to live.

The houses bore this out: all along the tree-shaded Bubbling Well Road, as it was called then, mansions aspiring to the air of the English country manor stood back upon their lawns. The neighbourhood was where the Europeans lived. Some of them might well have crossed swords with the man whom, ironically, Tibet Road for a time commemorated, by bearing his name. He was Yu Qiaqing, a chief protagonist in the May Thirtieth story, a man the Europeans would love to hate.

Few other men were as qualified to act as mediator between the Chinese community and the Municipal Council in the triple boycott of factory, school and shop that followed the killings. He was the president of the influential Shanghai General Chamber of Commerce, founder and managing director of the Sanbei Steam Navigation Company, and a man who had all the Shanghai merchants behind him. Best of all, he had been comprador to a number of Western firms, and knew barbarian ways better than anyone. He

Yu Qiaqing and family

came, like many of his kind, from the Ningbo region, that fount of entrepreneurial talent to the south of Shanghai. Born in 1863, he was to live in Shanghai for more than fifty years, becoming a financier and public figure of high standing.

Much of Shanghai's entrepreneurial muscle came from the comprador, a figure inextricably linked to the treaty port. From being Number One Boy in the European domestic household, the comprador had evolved into middleman, business associate and ultimately managing director of the foreign firm. He was paid a salary and expenses, but would also receive a commission for every deal he could swing. He smoothed the path of many a foreign trader, for he could speak pidgin English, bridge east-west differences, and was a fellow with many useful assets besides (not the least of which was the ability to bring himself to eat barbarian food if occasion demanded it). He had been a familiar figure on the Canton waterfront, and now he was responding to the Western commercial challenge in Shanghai. The comprador came nearer than any Chinese to catching the age's spirit of enterprise. By the end of the nineteenth century, there were few foreign business ventures that did not have some comprador money in them. They were the prototypes of that class of men which it is fashionable to term the national bourgeoisie, and of which Shanghai was the very source and bastion.

The compradors were without exception rich, but not at all cultured. Their commercial flair was acknowledged, not least along the bookish corridors of Chinese power, yet they were thought not altogether gentlemanly. Money eventually earned them gentility, as it had earned them political power. Still their Western ways and habits stood out like a sore thumb, and struck the snobbish sensibility as being in dreadfully poor taste. They were sneered at for aping the European, for thinking Foreign was best; one critic, the famous turn-of-the-century novelist Wu Jianren, even went so far as to say that "to the comprador, even a foreigner's fart is fragrant."

Yu Qiaqing, too, has been retrospectively denounced by left-wing historians as belonging to that unspeakably odious breed of men, the "comprador capitalist in the service of imperialism." But in fact there was far more to the man than that. In his day he was repudiated by the very imperialists that today he is thought to have been serving. The then British consul thought him "one of the most unscrupulous and anti-foreign of the local Chinese merchants whose companies were profiting enormously from the strike." And another Western observer called him "a thorough scoundrel," a man "suspected of communistic views ...."

4

To the south of where Nanking Road West crosses Taixing Road (previously Medhurst Road), there once stood, in what were then the outskirts of town, a well-tended park known to

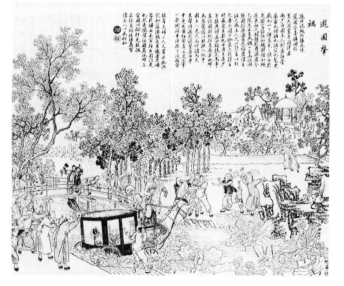

An accident in Zhang Gardens, 1893

the city's Chinese as Zhang Gardens. It has completely disappeared. But in its heyday it was where the very best folk in town came to loiter, genteel in silks and caps and fluttering fans. A large mansion in foreign design was set delectably behind a spacious park, lined thickly on both sides by tall and stately trees. Paths threaded their way through shrubs to where weeping willows trailed their tendrils about a lake. Here and there were benches for repose, and decorated pavilions for snacks and tea. There were slabs of gnarled ornamental rock about, and rare flowery shrubs that had come all the way from abroad. The park's owner had had a gaily painted pleasure boat brought over from Suzhou, and now it stood in the middle of the lake, the waters plashing gently against its sides, and catching the colourful image of its lanterns in the dusk. Girls of fifteen and sixteen acted as boatmen and bartenders, some working at the punt pole, others warming the wine. The crowds liked the gardens so much that they would linger till well after dark, when the lights would spangle, the singsong girls trill, and the occasional fireworks display or magic lantern show detain them right up to midnight.

It was in Zhang Gardens, in the years before the overthrow of the Manchu dynasty, that half the prelude to Shanghai's republican revolution was played out. In this city more than any other in China, student radicalism romantically thrived; here, fostered by papers like the *Su Bao*, which called the emperor a "young clown," the intelligentsia's progressive leanings found their most articulate expression. And it was in the hall of the gardens' Mansion of Quiet Joy (An Kai Di) that the gatherings of these young progressives were held — men like Cai Yuanpei, Zhang Taiyan, Zou Rong and Huang Zongyang, the Buddhist monk of Wumu Mountain. These were the men that got the famous Patriotic School going, and had it turned into a hotbed of revolution.

Cai Yuanpei and Zhang Taiyan were learned men, and wrote books and essays on scholarly subjects; the monk painted, and had a part-time meditative life; Zou Rong was absurdly young, wrote his impassioned treatise *Revolutionary Army* before he was 19, and was already martyred by the age of 21. The cause found its supporters among the business community too, and rich merchants gave generously to its resources. At a meeting called in the park to demonstrate against Russian designs on Manchuria in 1903, a diamond ring was found among the donations. The monk Zongyang had a patroness in Luo Jialing, the half-Chinese wife of Silas Hardoon, the millionaire Jew from Baghdad we have already glimpsed, and through her much money came the way of the cause.

But the young men were revolutionaries in principle rather than in practice. The crackdown on the *Su Bao* by the municipal authorities and the mysterious death of young Zou Rong in prison kept radical sentiments on the boil, as did the flow of subversive literature and "returned" Chinese students from Japan; but though there was a secret society and an assassin corps, and a bookstore appropriately acting as cover, still nobody could claim that the revolution was wrought by the Zhang Gardens crowd. When it did come, in 1911, it arrived by way of Wuchang. There, the rising which put the first torch to the pyre of the Manchu empire occurred on October 10, the date (the tenth day of the tenth month) which each subsequent Double Ten celebration would commemorate as the birth of the Chinese republic.

The Shanghai rising did not begin until the afternoon of November 3, and it was led by a conspirator called Chen Yingshi, the man whom Shanghai later honoured by raising a monument to his memory — a massive obelisk which has not survived — right in the heart of the Chinese city. It was he who led the raid upon the Shanghai arsenal. The attempt was unsuccessful, and Chen himself was captured, but then the army and police officers came over to the republican side, and the arsenal fell into revolutionist hands. The next day Shanghai was strung end to end with white flags, hung out of the Chinese houses to welcome the new regime. Shanghai was wholehearted in its enthusiasm for the republic: the students had clamoured for it; the businessmen had loosened their purse-strings for it, and even people in the theatrical world had had a share in the running of the show.

5

Further west, in a square flanked by Nanking Road West to the north and Middle Yan'an Road (formerly Avenue Foch) to the south, the Shanghai Industrial Exhibition Hall bears massively down upon its foundations. There is no suggestion at all of the gloriously personal eccentricities that were displayed all over this site only fifty years before. But a map of old Shanghai will tell us that the place was once called Hardoon Park, and should remind us of the legendary Jew whose magnificent private residence this was.

Hardoon (or Aili in Chinese) Park was approached through tall iron gates in painted vermilion. Into its 26 acres, Silas A.

Site of Hardoon Park

Hardoon and his wife Luo Jialing had packed a Buddhist hall, three separate residences, quarters for coveys of hangers-on and just about everything that nostalgic Chinese taste dictated — pavilions, rockeries, arched bridges, bamboo groves, artificial hills and lakes, vistas and classically inspired inscriptions. Here Mr and Mrs Hardoon lived in courtly splendour, surrounded by swarms of servants and ten adopted children, and devotedly attended by the lady's trusted major-domo — some say lover — Ji Juemi.

Hardoon spent his money lavishly on ancient paintings and manuscripts, and liked to think that scholars could engage in deeply learned dialogues in his house. In 1914 he established a school for Chinese children in Aili Park, where he could indulge his fancy for the ethos and ceremonials of a vanished Chinese past, for the pupils were nurtured on ancient games and Confucian proprieties, and a diet that would not offend even the strictest Buddhist vegetarian. When he himself died, in 1931, his funeral faithfully reproduced the rituals of both

Beth Aharon Synagogue

Jewish and Chinese obsequies, complete with a funeral oration composed by Zhang Taiyan, who by then had become one of the most august scholars of the day. In Hardoon Judaism had clearly been the lesser persuasion, even though he did, by his donation, build the Beth Aharon Synagogue on Museum Road. (This architecturally interesting building, with its combination of sharp corners and smooth curves, was subsequently turned into a museum. It may still be found on Huqiu Road, but with its top lopped off, its lower portion turned into a wall, and the rest reconstituted as a factory.)

Hardoon came to Shanghai as a penniless young man, worked as a night watchman in one of David Sassoon's warehouses, became a rent collector, and went on to make a staggering fortune in opium and real estate on his own. As the Chinese called raw opium *tu,* or earth, they were fond of saying, with an eye cocked at his acres and a pun in mind, that Hardoon's millions were made out of the clod. He was undoubtedly clever, had a good head for figures and a keen ear for languages. His contemporaries thought him eccentric: so obsessed was he with rent collecting that even after he had amassed a huge fortune, he would still go around the Chinese tenements himself to make sure that his poor tenants paid up on time. While his home was a palace his office was a hovel: there was no rug on the floor and no curtains at the windows, and even on Shanghai's coldest days, Hardoon would rather sit bundled up in his overcoat than install heating in the room. Yet he had the best curry cook in town and gave lavishly to his favourite charities. Many people in Shanghai hated him, and once an attempt was even made on his life. But he had an intelligence network and an Irish bodyguard, and a limitless run of very good luck. He made himself all respectable, sprucing up his image with endowments and civic activities, and simultaneously winning seats on the French and International Settlement Municipal Councils.

Aili, the name of his estate, stands for "Beloved Li," the

latter syllable taken from Mrs Hardoon's second name. Mrs Hardoon was a Eurasian, her father a French gendarme and her mother a Chinese from Fujian Province. Orphaned at nine, she lived in great poverty near the Old West Gate of the Chinese city, selling flowers and, some say, her sexual favours. She became a passionately devout Buddhist, encouraged in her ardour by the seductive power of Huang Zongyang, the Wumu Mountain monk we met earlier in

Mrs Hardoon

Zhang Gardens. The monk dreamed of overthrowing the throne, so Mrs Hardoon agreed to underwrite the necessary expenses, and even had his comrades to stay. For his part he placed his learning at her disposal, composing the literary inscriptions that graced the prospects and pavilions of the Hardoon Park. He persuaded her to undertake the printing of the Buddhist cannon, all 8,416 rolls of it, himself doing the editing. A picture of her appears in the first volume of the collection, showing her somewhat filled out by the years, and not at all the beauty she is widely thought to be.

Huang Zongyang retired after the fall of the empire to a monastery near Nanking, ousted from Mrs Hardoon's affections, the scandalmongers said, by the house-steward Ji Juemi. But when Hardoon died in 1931, and his wife a few years later, Ji was himself banished from the garden. The estate was divided among the childless couple's adopted children, to be dissipated by them in an all too familiar way. The direction of the heirs' pursuits prompted a contemporary observer to remark: "perhaps bars and brothels and gaming establishments sometimes perform useful functions by acting as channels for the redistribution of wealth."

During the Sino-Japanese war a fire broke out in Aili Park and all of the estate, save the plumbing of the fountain at the corner of the southern gates, went up in smoke. The place lingers now only in the memory, like some dream of vanished splendour, or some folly. Memories bind Silas Hardoon to Tongren Road, which many people still know as Hardoon Road. But for the most part his traces have been smothered by the heavily official air of the Shanghai Industrial Exhibition Hall, whose sheer awfulness is perhaps explained by its having originally been built as a monument to Sino-Soviet friendship. For an evocation of the sumptuous living enjoyed by the rich Jewish families in Shanghai, you have to go down the road, past the old bubbling well, to the massive building now known as the Children's Palace. "Palace" is no misnomer, for it is very grand, and was known in its heyday as the Marble House. It belonged to the Kadoorie family who, unlike Hardoon, are still a name to be reckoned with along the China coast.

Frenchtown

1

From a stretch of the waterfront wedged in between the International Settlement and the old Chinese city, the French Concession lapped over into the heart of Shanghai. It was crisscrossed with streets bearing the names of French dignitaries. These tended to fall into one of six categories. There were streets named after French envoys and ambassadors to China: Chongde Road, for example, was formerly named for Langrené, who came to Macao in 1844, and was France's very first envoy to China. Consuls have also left their mark: take Boulevard de Montigny, now Xizang or Tibet Road South, which derived its name from the founder of the French Concession, and its first consul. Yet another set of names came from the bigwigs on the Conseil d'Administration Municipal, Pichon being one, and Chapsal being another (these have been replaced by Fenyang Road and Danshui Road). The French Catholic priesthood was commemorated too: Rue Chevalier (now Jianguo Road), for example, was named for a priest working in the Xujiahui observatory established by the Jesuits at the southwestern corner of the concession. Another group of street names honoured French residents in Shanghai: among the best known of these was the clock and wine merchant Remi, who first came to Shanghai from Canton in 1848, and in no time at all was blazing a new trail here, the French flag tagging slyly along. Today Remi is forgotten, his street having been renamed Yongkang Road.

Perhaps the most incongruous of all were the names derived from famous French men at home. Corneille and Molière (now Gaolan and Xiangshan Road) gave their names to two short avenues leading in charming parallel from the green expanse of Fuxing Park (formerly the French Park). Avenue Joffre, now Huaihai Road, was named for the hero of the Marne. Route Vallon was named after the French aviator who flew the first aircraft to China. His Sommer mono- and bi-planes amazed the Shanghainese, to whom he gave a demonstration in the spring of 1911. He took off from the racecourse in the Jiangwan district to the north, but crashed

A street in the old French Concession

his aeroplane before he could land it on the racecourse to the south. The accident was a sad blow to French aplomb, and the stone raised in Vallon's memory in the French Park (which said of him that he was China's very first pilot, and that his courage and death added to the glory of France) had a touch of tragic anti-climax about it.

Today the French heritage has disappeared from the name plates, but in the streets there are mementoes still. The Chinese name for the plane trees shading the boulevards (which nowadays tend to be stuck all over with poles hung with washing) is still prefaced in Shanghai speech by the epithet "French," in recognition of the people who first planted them there. From the facades of buildings peel away the laundry and the pall of city dust, and you will find the substance of French architectural design underneath.

This is certainly true of Huaihai Road, or the Avenue Joffre of yesterday, which was to Frenchtown what Nanking Road was to the International Settlement. The Chinese used to say that there was a poetic flavour to it, by which they meant it felt rather French. You could shop for Parisian fashions there, or while away a lazy afternoon sipping coffee and eyeing the girls. The street was pre-eminently the haunt of the White Russians, those émigrés who had left Shanghai with perhaps the most enduring European legacy of all — the borsch soup that is today served in every Shanghainese restaurant in the world. Their other lasting contribution was to show up the entrenched Shanghailanders, to make the native realize that the white man was not always so posh after all. Before the Russians arrived in great numbers, these Europeans had kept successfully aloof from the natives, believing themselves naturally to be the superior breed. To them the Russian émigrés were a disgrace: the way they let the side down and fraternized with the natives, selling their services to all buyers, Chinese and European alike — the men as riding instructors and bodyguards, the women as hairdressers, dance hostesses and whores.

There was no better way to sample the ambience of Avenue Joffre than to saunter down to the Renaissance Café, tucked between the crossings at Rue Père Robert (now Ruijin Road II) and Avenue du Roi Albert (today's Shaanxi Road). You might find a Cossack in full regalia there, his breast-pockets studded with the phoney medals he had secretly bought from a Japanese-owned gimmick shop. You might eavesdrop on the other Russians there, telling everybody just how splendid life had been in Moscow or St Petersburg — for all the world as though they were real princes, generals and countesses. You might even come across Alexander Vertinsky, who had been desperately in love with Marlene Dietrich, and who had dedicated a poem to her about a hopeless passion for a movie star. In his day Alexander Vertinsky had been a great star himself, the toast of Tsarist Russia, enchanting his Moscow audiences with his songs of unrequited love and regret. He had come to Shanghai via Paris, New York and Hollywood, where penniless and unknown, he had had to sing to small immigrant audiences in low dives. He was eventually to leave Shanghai to return to the Soviet Union, invited back by Stalin himself, who used to play his recordings over and over again — great hits like *Magnolia* and *The Mad Organ Grinder* — so passionately did he adore Vertinsky's singing.

On the other hand you might simply come across an old friend — for the Renaissance was the sort of place where you bumped into people you knew — and spend the rest of the afternoon dawdling over gossip and a glass of barley water.

2

Eastward Avenue Joffre ran all the way to the edge of the Chinese city, becoming Rue Ningbo before it joined up with the Boulevard des deux Républiques. Rue Ningbo was appropriately named, for it skirted the grounds of the Ningbo Guild, the symbolic centre of the most powerful minority in Shanghai. Today the site is covered by the Taoyuan housing estate, and the strong parochial allegiances once embedded here are scattered.

In old Shanghai, business enterprise away from home was inconceivable without the contacts offered by the guild, a grouping of merchants based either on locality or on common trade. Traditionally, the guilds had always made for social welfare, for philanthropy: they opened schools and infirmaries, settled grievances, gave loans, took care of the aged and, whenever called for, provided coffins and cemetery space. The Ningbo Guild commanded ample burial grounds for its members in Shanghai, and in its prime was very rich and prestigious. Of all the settlers from the provinces, the Ningbo colony had contributed the most to Shanghai's commercial growth, transplanting to that city the skills and traditions that had once made Ningbo great. For at least five centuries before its eclipse by Shanghai, Ningbo had been the hub of a thriving coastal trade. Already in the thirteenth century, thousands of junks were thronging its shores, and

Ningbo Guild cemetery

when foreign trade flourished in the sixteenth century, a dazzling flow of silver from Japan, Portugal and Spain streamed through its harbour. It remained supreme right up to the first third of the nineteenth century; it certainly impressed a visiting British East India Company emissary, who wrote in his journal in 1832: "It surpasses anything Chinese which we have yet seen, in the regularity and magnificence of the buildings, and is behind none in mercantile fame."

When it began to be overshadowed by Shanghai, its natives migrated by the thousands, so infusing their adopted city with their daring and energy that nowadays, when the Chinese speak in awe of "Shanghainese" business acumen, they usually mean "Ningbo." They kept Shanghai stocked up with bankers, for their native place was rich in money experts, having itself fathered the traditional Chinese bank (the *qianzhuang*), and introduced it to the rest of China. Their other aptitude was for shipping, a logical development from their seafaring roots. Nor is the old flair dead: for proof one has only to remember Hong Kong's Sir Y.K. Pao — son of Ningbo, and today the biggest shipping magnate in the world.

Yu Qiaqing, encountered earlier in the role of the tough negotiator in the May Thirtieth conflict, was another Ningbo son. He first came to public notice in 1898, when he leapt to the defence of the Ningbo Guild when its graveyard was imperilled by a foreign power at the gates. The French had tried once before to take over the site by force. The Chinese had headed them off, but at the cost of losing half a dozen lives. A generation later, the French tried to possess the cemetery again, with plans to build a road, a school, a hospital and a slaughter-house on the site. Not allowing any soft scruples about venerating the dead to affect their purpose, nor recognizing the force of the emotions that had erupted in the past, they moved in troops to tear down the cemetery walls before the Guild had even had time to confer.

But the Ningbo community was neither slow to wrath nor hesitant in action. In a gesture unprecedented in the history of Chinese-foreign relations, they walked off their jobs, closed their shops, and for six whole months froze off all goods and services to the white community in Shanghai. It was the first time that the boycott had been used as a political instrument against the foreigner in China; a foretaste of Chinese recalcitrance to come, it was resoundingly successful: the French withdrew.

It will be recalled that Yu Qiaqing had a street named after him in Shanghai. He was not the only Ningbo native to be so honoured, however. Today's Xikou Road, off Yan'an Road East, was once named for Zhu Baosan, another eminent merchant from the region. But unlike Yu Qiaqing Road, which cut a wide swath across the face of Shanghai and was one of its leading thoroughfares, Rue Zhu Baosan was only 110 yards in length, and tainted with an unsavoury reputation. It was better known as Blood Alley, for it had been a place of drunken brawls and scabrous sailors on shore leave, where sozzled seamen from all over the world lurked in unsuspected corners, and the lights of smoky bars and low dives beckoned with lurid fascination. Nothing at all of the old flashiness survives today. The alley is now in a state of almost total dereliction, the downstairs part of once lovely buildings turned into workshops for broken down buses.

3

Because of its proximity to the Chinese quarter and its readiness to wink at forbidden activities, Frenchtown had always been a sanctuary for conspirators. It had been hospitable to Mao Zedong, who worked in Route Vallon (today's Nanchang Road) from 1924 to 1926. Zhou Enlai lived in the Concession in the early 1940s, his house on Rue Massenet (now Sinan Road) watched over by Kuomintang spies. Sun Yat-sen lived at 29 Rue Molière (today's Xiangshan Road), in a house with a garden and an arcaded portico at

Sun Yat-sen's residence

the back, opening through arches onto the lawns behind. It is still there, and may be visited as a museum.

Some people think Dr Sun Yat-sen overrated as a revolutionary, even if his compatriots do hail him as the father of the Chinese republic. Still his career was bound up with the overthrow of the Manchu throne, an addled power all patriotic Chinese were happy to see done away with. Impoverished, subjugated, overcrowded: such was the state of the nation on the eve of the revolution. There were plots and attempted assassinations, risings and subversive organizations. Students in Shanghai and Tokyo provided the latest political arguments, and overseas Chinese much of the money; businessmen were in it too, and army officers. Though the republican cause was loosely strung together, and not all its champions knew precisely what they were about, yet the revolution did carry the day. It needed little to shatter the crumbling empire, and in the end it took only a bomb explosion, and an accidental one at that, to send the

Manchus packing. It was in Wuchang, further up the Yangzi River, in a house where republican conspirators stored their grenades. The explosion not only gave the plot away, it alerted the police to the fact that many officers of the garrison were secretly republican party members. Realizing that their game was up, the officers forced their commander to choose between death or republicanism. The general chose the latter. Almost at once the monarchy was swept away in southern China. Sun Yat-sen was at the time raising funds in the USA, but he returned to China on Christmas Eve, 1911, to become the provisional president of the new republic.

The republic was established over the lower Yangzi, where one after another the provinces seceded from the empire and proclaimed their independence. But the north was not yet won. The strong man there was Yuan Shikai, creator of the famous Northern Beiyang Army, China's most powerful organized military force, from the ranks of whose officers would emerge the warlords of a later generation. The generals of that army were more Yuan's men than the emperor's. By stepping aside in Yuan's favour, Sun Yat-sen won him over to the republican cause. Invited to be president, Yuan manoeuvered the abdication of the emperor. Now he was in control, and dictatorship being far better suited to his style than democratic government, he turned parliament into a fiasco, a bluff. The shadow of political murder fell upon his enemies; one of them, Song Jiaoren, was assassinated while awaiting his train at Shanghai's North Station. The south tried to resist Yuan Shikai's grand design, staging a second revolution, but Yuan promptly quashed it, and Sun Yat-sen had to retreat swiftly to Japan.

In Shanghai the anti-Yuan revolutionists struck in the winter of 1915. Among the commanding officers was Chen Yingshi who, as we saw earlier, had delivered Shanghai over to the republic in the first place. Assuming command of the *Zhaohe*, a warship on the Huangpu River, Chen Yingshi and his officers — one of them was Chiang Kai-shek — made a bid for the arsenal and the Chinese quarter. It was a disaster from start to finish. As the revolutionists came storming towards the Chinese quarter, Yuan Shikai's troops and gunfire met them head-on; so heavy were the casualties that it was all they could do to retreat. Even that was difficult, for Yuan's men were all over Shanghai, and the revolutionary head-quarters in the French Concession was raided and policed that night. On the Huangpu, after firing an unpunctual and ineffective volley at the arsenal, the *Zhaohe* dithered, to be sprung upon early next morning by a barrage from two enemy ships, effectively sealing her doom. In the following year Chen Yingshi was found murdered by Yuan's thugs in an apartment at 14 Rue Chapsal. (Now known as Danshui Road, this street was for a time named Yingshi Road in his honour.)

Meanwhile Yuan's self-aggrandizement was becoming more and more apparent; the monarchy would be restored, it was decided, and he himself enthroned as emperor. The country was deeply sunk in malaise, but the dream of glory was far from over. Yet though the restoration was a saving fantasy for some, it was also a ludicrous delusion to others. In the end Yuan had to call it off, but on condition that he be made president for life. And now the supreme irony occurred: on the threshold of what might have been his great moment in life, in June 1916 Yuan Shikai died, and of perfectly natural causes.

An interlude of relative calm followed, but this rapidly disintegrated, and China was plunged into her warlord era, when political power splintered into deep provincial divisions, and near-independent militarist governors vied with each other for the richest prizes, like so many *condottieri*. Politically the scene was violent and muddled, but industrially and commercially it boomed for the bourgeoisie. First, there was the prosperity brought about by the world war: foreign competition was down and European demand was up. Then there was the growth of private enterprise, much stimulated by the rise in the price of silver (on which the Chinese currency was based), and the opening up of new markets abroad. Of course all this rested on cheap labour too, housed in suburbs like Pudong and Hongkou, and swelling to about a fifth of Shanghai's population by the end of the decade. Fresh blood ran in the Shanghai business community — young men recently returned from Columbia and other American universities, with the latest management methods at their fingertips, and itching to make their mark upon the scene.

In Rue Molière, Sun Yat-sen was being cultivated by emissaries from the Soviet Union. It was there too that Chiang Kai-shek first saw Soong Mayling, a meeting that would lead to their marriage in December 1927 in the ballroom of the splendid Majestic Hotel, where the bride, following European custom (as was fashionable among the westernized Chinese), wore white. The walls were hung with flowers and the wedding ceremony took place before a photograph of the late Sun Yat-sen, crossed below with the flags of nation and party in red, white and blue.

4

Beneath Shanghai's rich veneer, there festered a squalid layer. Through the city had always streamed a dreary flow of poor people — peasants from the countryside, refugees from war or natural calamities, vagrants in search of work — and these were forming into an embryo proletariat with the swelling numbers of coolies and factory workers. For these, brutally harsh working conditions and hideous overcrowding were part of the day's struggle and experience of Shanghai. The poverty would get worse: in 1937 the Municipal Council of the International Settlement collected over 20,000 corpses from the streets — homeless people who had simply starved or frozen to death. It was for its heartlessness in the face of such terrible conditions that Shanghai later earned its unwholesome reputation.

Though most of Shanghai did not know it yet, revolu-

Taking the sun outside the venue of the Chinese Communist Party's first national congress

tionary cells were already forming, and in July 1921, at a meeting at 76 Xingye Road (previously 106 Rue Wantz), the Chinese Communist Party formally came into being. The venue was the home of one of the delegates. Today it is a museum, and visitors may see the conference room in supposedly its original state, complete with ashtrays (two) and teacups (twelve). The delegates, Mao Zedong included, are said to have put up nearby at the Bo Wen Girls School at 127 Taicang Road (formerly 389 Rue Auguste Boppe), the girls themselves being on vacation at the time. The proceedings had some fraught moments, as when the French police broke in and made a search. In order to avoid further harrassment the delegates decided to repair to a lake near Hangzhou, where they rented a houseboat and completed their business in peace. Afterwards Shanghai was infiltrated everywhere by communist workers, for it seemed then to be much the best place in which to start a revolution: Marxist theory demanded an industrial proletariat, and Shanghai was the only city in China that could offer a sizeable one.

5

The gaiety of Shanghai in the decades before its fall is something which almost all elderly reminiscences evoke. There were films from Hollywood, plays and recitals, cabarets and Peking operas, and opening nights when society turned out in all its scented finery. The Shanghai Art Theatre, standing at 57 Maoming Road South (formerly Rue Cardinal Mercier), was witness to such glittering scenes. So was the Cercle Sportif Français (now the Jinjiang Club), standing diagonally opposite, where music once played in the cocktail hour and dinner dances swung to the latest rhythms deep into the night.

The Shanghai Art Theatre is a pale shadow of its former self, which was the famous Lyceum Theatre, a favourite haunt of the British residents. Home of the Shanghai Amateur Dramatic Society, the Lyceum was the first

Jinjiang Club

Shanghai Art Theatre

European theatre to be built in Shanghai. It began life in 1867, in a wooden building just off the Bund. When fire destroyed it, a new building was promptly put up, and in its domed auditorium, visiting opera companies and ballet troupes, and orchestras and circuses from Europe and the United States performed to enthusiastic audiences. The building on Maoming Road, the third and last home of the Amateur Dramatic Club, was completed in 1931, and opened in the February of that year to a glittering assembly, with the British Consul-General officiating. As tastes changed and new forms of entertainment came to Shanghai, the theatre began alternating stage plays with film screenings, kicking off in the latter category with Kay Francis in *Girl About Town*.

The Shanghailanders took as avidly to greyhound racing. It became all the rage in the late 1920s, no less than three dog tracks opening in the European part of town. There was Luna Park in the International Settlement; there was the Stadium; grandest of all, there was the Canidrome at the intersection of Avenue du Roi Albert (the Shaanxi Road of today) and Route Hervé de Siéyès (now Yongjia Road). It opened in November 1928 in an atmosphere so heady, and to a crowd so excited by its stands of 50,000 capacity, its large training ground and kennels, its luxurious dining rooms and ballroom, that it was as if they were cheering home the winners already. For some it was indeed a place of the sweetest triumph, as their dogs zipped past the winning post first; for others it spelt harsh reality, as hopes of victory were dashed and money went down the drain. Today the Canidrome has been turned into a centre of tamer entertainment called Culture Square.

Another sport pursued with passion in the old days was *jai alai*, a game derived in the Basque country of Spain from handball. It is an eminently watchable game, and spectators often sat spellbound before the *fronton*, as the *jai alai* court is called, while the players hurled the *pelota* (the ball) about.

But even more to the taste of the Shanghai patrons was the fact that it was a game in which you could lay bets.

Nowhere was old Shanghai's taste for vulgar pleasure more completely satisfied than in the Great World, a rollicking amusement centre standing at the point where Tibet Road meets Yan'an Road (the Avenue Edouard VII of old). The crowds that visit it today are still stupendous, but the name has been changed to Shanghai Youth Palace, and the place is no longer a vice spot, where no young girl dared venture into alone, unless she were of the oldest profession on earth. We have been left a vivid description of it by the Hollywood film director Josef von Sternberg, who visited it in the mid-1930s, and recorded his impressions in his memoirs *Fun in a Chinese Laundry:*

"The establishment had six floors to provide distraction for the milling crowd, six floors that seethed with life and all the commotion and noise that go with it, studded with every variety of entertainment Chinese ingenuity had contrived.

Shanghai Youth Palace

When I had entered the hot stream of humanity, there was no turning back had I wanted to. On the first floor were gambling tables, singsong girls, magicians, pick-pockets, slot machines, fireworks, bird cages, fans, stick incense, acrobats and ginger. One flight up were the restaurants, a dozen different groups of actors, crickets in cages, pimps, midwives, barbers, and earwax extractors. The third floor had jugglers, herb medicines, ice-cream parlours, photographers, a new bevy of girls their high-collared gowns slit to reveal their hips, in case one had passed up the more modest ones below who merely flashed their thighs; and under the heading of novelty, several rows of exposed toilets, their impresarios instructing the amused patrons not to squat but to assume a position more in keeping with the imported plumbing. The fourth floor was crowded with shooting galleries, *fan-tan* tables, revolving wheels, massage benches, acupuncture and moxa cabinets, hot-towel counters, dried fish and intestines, and dance platforms serviced by a horde of music makers competing with each other to see who could drown out the others. The fifth floor featured girls whose dresses were slit to the armpits, a stuffed whale, story tellers, balloons, peep shows, masks, a mirror maze, two love-letter booths with scribes who guaranteed results, 'rubber goods' and a temple filled with ferocious gods and joss sticks. On the top floor and roof of that house of multiple joys a jumble of tightrope walkers slithered back and forth, and there were seesaws, Chinese checkers, mah-jongg, strings of firecrackers going off, lottery tickets, and marriage brokers. And as I tried to find my way down again an open space was pointed out to me where hundreds of Chinese, so I was told, after spending their coppers, had speeded the return to the street below by jumping from the roof." It was indeed, as von Sternberg puts it, a "condensed world."

The amusement complex was owned by Huang Chujiu, a Shanghai drugstore proprietor known for his miracle potion for toning up the brain. He made a fortune on this wonder drug, which was recognized everywhere by the brand name "Yellow" and the photograph of Mr Huang's Jewish friend on the packet (a European face, in those days, bore the stamp of authenticity). The Great World was eventually to pass into the hands of another Shanghai big shot, Huang Jinrong, the underworld chief of whom we shall be hearing more later.

6

Huang Jinrong's story is inextricably linked to that of Du Yuesheng. The latter was of the very essence of old Shanghai. With his rags-to-riches life history, his shady ties to the underworld, his taint of scandal and his high style of living, Du Yuesheng exemplified better than anyone the opportunities and moral ambiguities of his age. His traces are embedded in the French Concession, which had been his base; the interested visitor may look in at the Donghu Hotel on Donghu Road, for example, and imagine it as it used to be

Donghu Hotel

— home of mobsters and den of thugs. Its address was 26 Rue Doumer then, and in its day it had been an opium warehouse, a movie studio, and even the temporary retreat of a deposed president. The house had been acquired by Du in 1923, and thoroughly redecorated to house Li Yuanhong, Yuan Shikai's successor as president of the Chinese republic, after he had been jockeyed out of office by other warlords. After the second world war it passed into the hands of the United States government, which paid Du, so people say, US$450,000 for it. Du himself did not live there, having built another mansion on Rue Wagner (now Ninghai Road West), and there had comfortably installed his three wives (one on each floor), nine cars, eighteen chauffeurs, three bodyguards and droves of servants.

It is difficult to distil the facts of DuYuesheng's life from folklore, so steeped is he in Mafia-like mystique, and so much was he part of the cloak-and-dagger subculture of smugglers, kidnappers, terrorists, extortioners and revolutionists, which by definition is shrouded in murky secrecy. But whatever may have been the true character of the Shanghai Mafia, Du Yuesheng was undoubtedly its godfather. In the prime of his career he became a philanthropist, a pillar of Shanghai's business community and the confidant of politicians and national leaders, yet to the end he remained dependent on mob muscle.

He began life on the wilder shores of the Chinese El Dorado, in a village in Pudong on the wrong side of the Huangpu River. For most of his childhood his father was away in Yangshupu, a district to the north of the Suzhou Creek, struggling to keep his rice shop open. Life was hard, and became even harder when, one after the other, his mother, his father and his stepmother died. After some years of hanging about street corners, getting into scrapes, gambling with the local layabouts and squeezing the last penny out of what remained of the family property, he struck out, aged fifteen, for the bright lights of the big metropolis.

He found himself at the hub of the French Bund, in 1902 a place of sweating coolies, bulging godowns, swerving handcarts, smelly cargoes, ships loading and unloading, river steamers, junks, lighters, milling crowds and roaring trade. He became apprenticed to one fruiterer, then to another. He found his friends among the waterfront urchins and his pleasures in a back-alley game of craps. Gambling was to

Du Yuesheng

become a lifelong passion, and even long after he had graduated from the back-alley bet to the white linen-covered mah-jongg table, he would proudly recall his first win at a low gambling den, an unforgettable triumph for a lad of thirteen.

Through knowing touts and small-scale hoods he was recruited to the ranks of the Green Gang, a secret society which, like the Mafia, had historically been a patriotic fraternity and which initiated its members in time-honoured ceremonies with oaths and symbolic acts. Like the Mafia too, it specialized in enterprises like drug-peddling and gambling, businesses in which the enormous profits bought official connivance, but also attracted gangland rivalry and violence. The French Concession harboured a roaring opium trade, the highest-ranking Chinese officer in the gendarmerie having a bigger stake in it than anyone. He was Huang Jinrong, running with the hare and hunting with the hounds. The French had cynically recognized the world of Shanghai for what it was, a jungle of bums, adventurers, opportunists and swindlers, where one culture had to dictate to another with neither side remotely understanding the other. To the French there were worse sins to a police force than having as its Chinese head a man who, by virtue of his influence in the underworld, kept the level of crime from brimming over. It was the familiar symbiosis between crime and the law, with handsome rake-offs for everyone.

Du Yuesheng's meeting with Pockmarked Huang, as he was often called, marked a watershed in his life, for it was after he had become a member of the Huang *ménage* that his career took off, helped in the earlier phase by Huang's wife, whose confidence he had won from the start. One of Du's most celebrated coups was to make gangland safe for opium. Because of the warring factions in the underworld, a consignment of opium suffered high risks of being hijacked by a rival gang at nearly every point in its passage from the ship to the warehouse. With immense skill and assurance, Du seized on a profit-sharing plan of operation which ended the banditry once and for all, and achieved a lasting peace in the underworld.

A life of increasing political importance followed. By setting Green Gang toughs upon the communists in the 1927 uprising, he helped Chiang Kai-shek secure Shanghai for the Kuomintang. He was a supremely gifted arbitrator, and could be counted on by the Chinese, French and British alike to step in whenever there was a whiff of trouble in the air. There was no communist that could not be put out of action, no strike that could not be controlled. He became a dedicated nationalist, his sympathies reaching perhaps their clearest expression in the Sino-Japanese war when, even while sojourning in Hongkong, he continued to preside over resistance work in Shanghai. He donated a bullet-proof car to the commander defending Pudong, and offered to sink a whole fleet of ships under his control so as to block the Japanese vessels in the Yangzi River.

He had immense power, and he wielded it liberally. One of his favourite phrases was "you have my word," an undertaking guaranteed by his reputation and sense of honour, and so absolute that no other form of assurance was necessary. He vouched for his friends and answered for his deeds, and like the secret-society man that he was, looked upon all accepted obligations as supremely binding. He disdained paltriness in any form and never did anything by half-measures. He did not like being crossed and would show his displeasure by sending a coffin round in the morning the way other people send flowers. When he gambled, he knew neither night nor day. He liked to sweep flamboyantly through Shanghai in his huge bullet-proof car, with a couple of diamond-spangled singsong girls by his side and an army of bodyguards all around, and the feeling of all Shanghai at his feet.

In 1931 the French elected him to the Municipal Council. Socially he had clearly "arrived" by 1933 when, decked with directorships and honours, he attained a fulsome entry in the Shanghai *Who's Who:* "Better known as: Dou Yu-seng. Born 1887; native of Shanghai. Entered business at an early age. At present most influential resident, French Concession, Shanghai. Well-known public welfare worker. 1932, councillor, French Municipal Council. President, Chung Wai Bank, and Tung Wai Bank, Shanghai. Founder and Chairman, board of directors, Cheng Shih Middle School. President, Shanghai Emergency Hospital. Member, supervisory committee, General Chamber of Commerce. Managing director, Hua Feng Paper Mill, Hangchow. Director, Commercial Bank of China, Kiangsu and Chekiang Bank, Great China University, Chinese Cotton Goods Exchange, and China Merchants Steam Navigation Co., Shanghai, etc., President, Jen Chi Hospital, Ningpo."

Yet he was tagged with a humble past that did not fit in with present grandeur and eminence. He took pains to appear gentrified in manner and dress, and not even on the hottest day in summer would he be seen with the collar of his Chinese robe unbuttoned. Once he had proudly sported a 4½-carat diamond ring upon his finger, but when it struck him at a banquet that none of the high officials and dignitaries present wore one, he removed it as soon as he was home and never put it on again. And only his very closest intimates knew that he had an indigo tattoo of an anchor above his right wrist. In 1938 the English writers W.H. Auden and Christopher Isherwood met him, and their description of his appearance in their book *Journey to A War* suggests that he did become a man of an enigmatic presence: "Du himself was tall and thin, with a face that seemed hewn out of stone, a Chinese version of the Sphinx. Peculiarly and inexplicably terrifying were his feet, in their silk socks and smart pointed European boots, emerging from beneath the long silken gown. Perhaps the Sphinx, too, would be even more frightening if it wore a modern top-hat." They talked entirely of the Red Cross, of which Du was a board director.

He barely survived the passing of old Shanghai, dying in 1951 in Hong Kong. Today, to conjure up the temper of old Shanghai, one has only to mention his name, so inseparable was he from the greed, the lawlessness, the vulgarity, the swank and the bizarreness of that unique society.

A Miscellany

1

Those who have a bent for historical places and a desire to poke about in streets and corners in search of the past will find many more relics of old Shanghai. Here is where the May Fourth Movement took wings; there, China's greatest modern writer spent his last days; here Buddhist superstitions thrived, there Roman Catholicism reigned. Upon this site young poets had been martyred, from that soil a westernized intelligentsia had grown.

The wanderer in search of these miscellaneous relics may begin at the Hunan (South Shanghai) Stadium lying sandwiched between Daji Road and Fangxie Road to the west of the Chinese quarter. This was where, on May 7, 1919, a crowd of 20,000 gathered, marking a historical moment of anguish and awakening. The crowd held flags, bearing emotive legends — "Give us back our country," for instance. Only three days before, on May 4, thousands of students had marched to the Square of Heavenly Peace in Peking to demonstrate against the ignominy at the Peace Conference in Versailles.

The world war had come to an end and China, having been pressured into fighting it, now sent her delegation to the conference along with the other victor countries. At the conference China demanded the surrender of the privileges in Shandong province which Germany had wrested from her in 1897. But her hopes were rudely dashed when it was learnt that the Western Allies had already secretly transferred the German rights to Japan. The Chinese public, when it heard the news on the wire, was stunned at the betrayal. Three thousand students from Peking universities marched in impassioned protest, bearing slogans like "China belongs to the Chinese," "Boycott Japanese goods," "Down with the traitors" and so on. It was an orderly and sombre demonstration to begin with, and spectators wept in anguish and sympathy as they watched the students march past. But later a pro-Japanese politician was beaten up and pelted with salted eggs (which happened to be handy), and tussles with the police led to the arrest of dozens of students and the

May 31 gathering

death of one. Word reached Shanghai the next day, and there the students set about organizing a strike. In a colossal show of strength and solidarity, 100,000 students and citizens turned up on May 31 at a memorial meeting for the martyred Peking student; stirring speeches were made, white flags waved from doors in mourning, tall white banners rose over the crowds, bearing legends choked with emotion. From that moment Shanghai became the centre of the May Fourth Movement, as it came to be known in history.

One thing led to another. By June the student strikes and boycotts had become a staggering wave with supporters from nearly every walk of life. Never had the student been more persuasive, never had his speeches fired greater response. Thousands of tradesmen were won over to the cause, closing their shops in sympathetic protest. If they hesitated, the students would fall on their knees with ritual solemnity, and weep. Almost every day there were minor incidents. When a rice shop in the Chinese quarter refused to close, four to five students implored the proprietor on their knees. When a shop assistant tried to chase them off, an outraged bystander started pelting the shop with stones. Soon a mob gathered, and when at last the owner himself appeared, they set upon him and pulled off half his beard. Then the police appeared and rounded them all up, quickly dousing their patriotic fervour.

Yet the demonstrators did not, by and large, resort to violence. They were only doggedly determined. They were all around the main streets, putting up posters and circulating handbills, and if the authorities stripped one bill off a wall, up would spring another. The jingle pasted on the facade of a barber shop at the corner of Fujian and Jiujiang Road may stand as representative of this persistence:

"Stripping and sticking,
You strip, I stick;
You do the stripping,
I do the sticking;

Just you strip,
I'll just stick;
If again you strip,
Then again I'll stick;
If you really must strip,
Then I really must stick;
You stick to your stripping,
And I'll stick to my sticking;
One bill, two bills, strip them off all,
Thousands and ten thousands I'll stick up every wall."

On the morning of June 5, a strike begun by Shanghai's shopkeepers in the Chinese city snowballed through Frenchtown and the International Settlement, flattening all life and commerce out of them. Never had the marketplace looked more like a ghost town. Soon the factories were infected, and over 70,000 workers walked off their jobs. So thoroughly fired was the public by the passions of the movement that even beggars, pickpockets and prostitutes went on strike. The beggar kings and underworld bosses gave the order for their following to refrain from normal business for the duration of the demonstration, and petty crime abated for days. It was an extraordinarily united movement, and afterwards, whenever Shanghai looked back on it, it would wonder at the scale, the heroism, and the sheer sweep of it all. The American philosopher John Dewey, who had arrived in China in time to see it unfold, was certainly a good deal impressed, and wrote in a letter home that "we are witnessing the birth of a nation, and birth always comes hard ... To think of kids in our country from fourteen on, taking the lead in starting a big cleanup reform politics movement and shaming merchants and professional men into joining them. This is some country." The movement subsided after a few months, but it had touched politics, language, literature and the position of women; it had paved the way for change, and given the old society a violent shake. And though China did not perhaps know it yet, from the May Fourth generation would presently spring the great shapers of her future destiny.

2

Strong social and literary currents had formed the backdrop to the May Fourth Movement. Intellectual horizons were being widened, as yet larger areas of the Western world were unfolded before Chinese eyes, and while one section of the public devoured the lurid exposés in the gutter press, another lapped up translations of Western literature. A leftwing journal had been founded in Shanghai in 1915, and now its name — *Xin Qingnian* to some, *La Jeunesse* to others — was on the lips of every student. From its columns would come words like *bolshevism* and *Marxism*, and ideas that set young hearts on fire.

From a historical distance we can survey the intellectual scene. We can see the urgent jostle of new thoughts for expression, the experimentation with new literary forms to clothe these thoughts. We see Lu Xun, who in his creation of the fictitious character Ah Q came nearer than anyone to capturing that combination of bluster and servility that was so often the Chinese response to authority, standing head and shoulders above the contemporary writers, and setting his stamp upon the scene.

Lu Xun moved to Shanghai with his wife in October 1927 and lived there until his death in 1936. His only child was born the year after their arrival in Shanghai. Lu Xun named him for the city, calling him Haiying or Child of Shanghai. Today Lu Xun's memory is honoured in the Lu Xun Mausoleum and Memorial Museum in Hongkou Park, and in the house where he died in Shanyin Road, where homely souvenirs—a desk, some books in a cupboard, a bed and some chairs — evoke his unostentatious life. Books were a solace in his last years, as was the friendship of men like Kanza Uchiyama, the Japanese owner of a bookshop on Sichuan Road North. Hongkou was Little Tokyo, the heart

九月十三日
一九三三年

Lu Xun and family, 1933

Kanza Uchiyama's bookshop

of the 20,000-strong Japanese community in Shanghai, and Lu Xun, who had studied in Japan, mixed easily with these foreign residents. After 1937 the Japanese were to be much more aggressively established in Hongkou and in the adjacent Zhabei, their shellfire and machine guns making these rather depressing areas even more dismal.

To visit the Lu Xun Museum is to conjure up his ten years in Shanghai, a time alive with literary debate and the comings and goings of writers. Revered traditions were no longer being clung to, but seen by a younger generation as something that choked the life out of Chinese culture as a creeper saps a tree. But what should replace them? Bourgeois or proletarian literature; art for art's sake, or art for life's sake; the colloquial language or the classical written style: the air buzzed with such controversies. The inspiration of these men was often patriotic, and sometimes Marxist. They felt it necessary to be engaged in politics, that they were moving into some deeply significant social condition. All would have been fine had they moved from vision to understanding, but often their revolutionary fervour was a dam against real experience, and this made the products of their pens read like the outpourings of breast-beating adolescents.

We meet them perhaps at a coffee shop on Sichuan Road North, or at the Golden Theatre staging a progressive play, or perhaps at Shanghai College, a place so communist that the authorities closed it. Some of them will be drunk with the lyricism of the advancing masses; others will fancy themselves China's answer to Ibsen. Yet others will, under the impact of the new theoretical sexual freedom, wallow in the sweet agonies of romantic love. Often the sentiments were too swollen, the expression too inflated. Their writing made a perfect butt for Lu Xun's biting lampoons. The radical revolutionary literature adopted by the Creation Society (a literary clique) was simply worthless, he said. He referred to a poem by one of the poets of the day, which had everywhere been banned, and said that it was "written in the International Settlement in Shanghai where he looked out towards revolutionary Canton ... his PONG, PONG, PONG in ever larger type merely showing the impressions made on him by Shanghai film posters and advertisements for soya sauce."

In the popular market, there were at least a hundred magazines catering to more feminine tastes. For writers of novelettes and short stories, these magazines served a purpose rather like penny periodicals did in Victorian England. And like such fiction, these stories depended for their appeal on such irresistible themes as thwarted love, scandal, crime and passion and vice. Shanghai, of course, abounded in the latter, and it quite naturally became the setting for every tale of exposure. The prototypes of such writing went back a long way, but the changes that had been wrought in Chinese society, and which this fiction reflected, gave the old themes a new twist. Love was never the same again after the May Fourth Movement, which threw the antique conventions out of the window and made it possible for young people in China to contemplate, for perhaps the first time in their lives, marriages based not on parental choice and decree, but on romantic love — a possibility utterly inconceivable before. It was as if a lid had been lifted, and every young heart that was wrung with this new emotion was pouring it out. The immense taste for romance made the magazines runaway bestsellers. On the morning that the weekly *Saturday* came out, readers would already be waiting outside the distributor's shop in Canton Road before it opened. The magazine had so much currency that its title, which apparently was inspired by the American evening weekly of the same name, became part of the glossary of literary terms, "Saturday school" being a synoym for romantic fiction. (Another term for it, coined in 1920 at a gathering of writers at a restaurant on Hankou Road, was "Lovebirds and Butterfly school.") Strictly speaking, the genre is not exclusive to Shanghai, but it was in Shanghai that it reached the peak of its growth and popularity.

In his 1929 essay on Shanghai literature, Lu Xun traces its development. There had always been a vogue in boy-meets-girl stories in China, the boy traditionally a gifted scholar, the girl a ravishing beauty. This got elaborated, says Lu Xun, in Shanghai, where the beauty that was readiest to hand was the whore. And so there evolved the familiar scenario of the gifted scholar being loved by the tender-hearted whore, and their living happily ever after. But while this was all very well in theory — the theory that only a scholar could be enamoured of a fallen woman, and it took a prostitute to cherish a hapless scholar — reality was infinitely more mundane, and soon it was discovered that it was not the scholar's genius that the whore was after, but his money. This was hardly palatable to the reading public, and so another scenario had to be devised where not only was the scholar not duped by the whore, it was she who was the pushover. The stories which related how this happened enjoyed huge popularity, since they could be used as a guide to whoring. In such stories the scholar was a hero who got the better of

A Shanghai lady, 1861-64

harlots — in other words a scholar with a touch of the thug. He became a model for the movies, where the anti-hero was a smooth type who, like the Shanghai city slicker, knew his way around the arts of philandering and scrounging — but was a good guy for all that.

In time the scholar-ruffian novel went out of fashion, partly because, thinks Lu Xun, the cliché became dreadfully overworked. Presently a new crop of books appeared, and began setting a new trend. The stories were still of the scholar-beauty type, but now the beauty was a girl from a good family; she and her scholar would be seen mooning about, quite unable to part, in the shade of a willow tree, or under the blossoms of a flowering shrub, like a pair of butterflies, or a couple of Mandarin ducks (traditionally the symbol of inseparable lovers). But sometimes their love would be doomed, either because their parents were stern or the girl was born unlucky.

Today, if you are lucky, you might still find a copy of the latest reissue of the novel *Qiu Haitang,* that perfect example of the genre, left in the bookshops. Alternately a newspaper serialization, a stage play and a film, *Qiu Haitang* (which translates as Begonia and is the name of the hero, a male Peking Opera singer of female roles) is so much part of the memorabilia of old Shanghai that the era would be inconceivable without it. The heroine is a paragon of womanly virtue, forced into concubinage by a brutal warlord. She and Qiu Haitang fall in love. Growing more unspeakably vicious by the chapter, the warlord and his henchmen do everything in their power to destroy the liaison, finally disfiguring Qiu Haitang's face and ruining his career as an opera star. Qiu Haitang flees to the country, there to live a gruelling and anonymous life as a farmer. The heroine tracks him down after a lapse of more than ten years, but reaches him only in time to see him die.

The dramatic possibilities of the story were quickly apparent, and were indeed most successfully exploited by the theatre and the cinema. The stage adaptation opened at the Carlton (now the Changjiang Theatre at 21 Huanghe Road) in December 1942 and ran for 135 days, breaking all records. Audiences thrilled to the stage translation of scenes like the following, in which Qiu Haitang meets the heroine for the first time. "... Another wait of three to four minutes, then the sound of light footsteps, and there entered a young lady of the lightest and plainest toilet. Cursory were the looks which she and Qiu Haitang exchanged, but great was the sense of unexpectedness that struck both at once. Of the two, Qiu Haitang's surprise was the more acute, for she had already heard her husband extol Qiu Haitang's performances and his many singular activities. Why else would she deign to come and meet him? Still she could not but wonder at the simplicity of his attire and the perfect propriety and rectitude of his bearing; it seemed almost inconceivable that this was the darling of the theatre world, the opera star.

"For his part, nothing about the lady's looks and dress was what he had expected. Of concubines in rich households, he had perhaps seen far too many; always there was that bewitching aura of the seductress. Even married ladies like Manager Wang's daughter-in-law can sometimes be a trifle fast, however ordinary may be the families they come from. Yet the lady that now stands before him — how utterly grave, and how quietly elegant; the beauty, undeniably, is of the highest order; yet the dignity — oh the dignity — can scarcely be surpassed."

Never had Shanghai theatre-goers been more captivated. Many of them, having seen the play several times, knew the dialogues by heart and anticipated all the lines, mouthing the words with the actors during the performance. There had never been a better tear-jerker, and during the scene in which the hero died, none, not even the men, could look on dry-eyed. The play was so successful that at one time six others imitating it were running simultaneously in Shanghai.

3

A frequent visitor to Lu Xun's house in the late 1920s was a bespectacled young writer called Rou Shi, chiefly remembered for his novelette *February* (which was made into a successful film), and for being one of the Five Martyrs executed by the Kuomintang during the witch-hunt days. On the night of February 7, 1931, Rou Shi and four other writers — Hu Yepin, Feng Keng, Li Weisen and Yin Fu — faced the firing squad in Longhua, on the outskirts of Shanghai, along with eighteen other communists. After the blitz on communists in Shanghai in 1927, death tailed hundreds of revolutionaries to that southwestern corner of Shanghai, where the Kuomintang garrison headquarters snuffed out their lives with bland despatch.

The youngest of the Five Martyrs was barely 21, the oldest not more than 29. They had been present at a clandestine meeting in the International Settlement's Eastern Hotel on

Rou Shi

Tibet Road, had been pounced upon by the British police and handed over to the Kuomintang authorities. Perhaps because they were writers, their arrest prompted the disapproval of the Western press, which saw them as "the flower of their generation," most cruelly nipped in the bud. Their bodies were exhumed after Shanghai's liberation in 1949 and moved from Longhua to the Martyrs' Cemetery to the north of the city. But the ghosts of many an anonymous hero still hover in the shadows in Longhua. A local guidebook reminds the citizens that it was here that countless had died for the revolution; "so when spring fills the air," it goes on to say, "and the peach trees are ablaze with blossom," when, with the advent of the fifth solar term (by tradition the time for sweeping the graves), people's thoughts turn naturally to the dead, then these heroes too will be sadly remembered, and deeply mourned.

Yet it is not in the martyred dead, nor even in its peach blossoms, that the fame of Longhua chiefly lies. When the people of Shanghai set out for Longhua, it was to wander through the halls of the Buddhist monastery there, to clamber up to the top of its ancient pagoda, rising high above the curving roofs, and to look out from there to the river and country beyond.

Buddhism made great headway in Shanghai after the Song dynasty, when twenty-seven monasteries were added to the two existing ones. Their number increased progressively down the centuries, and Shanghai sheltered at least a hundred before the last dynasty fell. Most have disappeared without a trace. The Longhua monastery, too, has had its ups and downs, now devastated by fire, now ravaged by insurgents, and has been rebuilt several times. Its history goes back 1,733 years, and its powers were said to be magical. Some claimed for the pagoda powers of cure and protection, for the place was the habitat of dragons; these supernatural creatures rid the waters of poisonous essences, and kept the devotees safe from feared disease. Another legend revolves round a bowl of water kept underneath the summit of the pagoda; a pair of sacred carp splashed about in it, but the bowl never ran dry. In the sixteenth century a monk lived in the pagoda, and it was his wont to sit in his room all day not uttering a word. One night he suddenly spoke: "What a nerve!" he bellowed. "Who is stealing our treasure?" And out he went like a shot, brandishing his staff. When he reached the courtyard he took a flying leap into the air and vanished. Presently he turned up at the pagoda again, and told his attendants that he had chased the thief to the edge of the Wusong River, and there had bludgeoned the thief with his staff. The thief fled, dropping the bowl of carp into the water. Some time after the event a fisherman claimed he spotted the bowl under the water at low tide, but not even the combined strength of scores of men was enough to lift it out again.

Popular religion has long lost its force in Shanghai, but the Yu Fo or Jade Buddha Temple in Anyuan Road has not completely degenerated into a mere tourist spectacle. On

Jade Buddha Temple

Chinese New Year's Day, the first day of the lunar calendar, the temple is open to the local citizens for the offering of incense and the performance of devotions. The old men in monkish robes that you see wandering about the courtyard are more tourist guide than cleric, but they know a thing or two about Buddhism, and transliterations of Sanskrit names in the Shanghai vernacular fall glibly and convincingly from their lips.

The interest and richness of the temple come from its two supremely rare statues of Śākyamuni Buddha, presented to a Chinese monk during a pilgrimage to Burma in 1882. Before the Yu Fo Temple was completed in 1918, they were housed in a monastery in the northern suburb of Jiangwan. Each is carved from a single piece of creamy jade, and is startling in its marmoreal beauty. In box-cases of glass, one sits, the other reclines; both have the bump of wisdom on the top of the head and the long flapping earlobes about the shoulders. They wear diadems set in jewels and kindly smiles on their

Reclining Jade Buddha

Seated Jade Buddha

Hall of Diamond Kings in Yu Fo Temple

ruby-red lips. To the altars there clings an aura of heavy opulence, gilded, polished and silken. Going into the temple is like coming upon a cache of treasures — stone and carved wood Bodhisattvas, ancient bronze tripods and Buddhist icons, scrolls of handwritten sutras dating from very early times, and the gigantic gilded figures of the Diamond Kings of Heaven looming up to the left and the right.

The temple stands touchingly for the present regime's concession — with an eye on the tourist trade — to "Chinese tradition." Perhaps the exhibits are on loan from defunct temples and monasteries elsewhere. Still, the offerings of fruit and cakes on the altars stir memories of past time, when for many of the local populace gods and goblins existed, and had to be propitiated by overtures to the stomach.

4

In Shanghai there are many reminders that Christianity was for generations a strong contestant for the devotion of the citizenry. Though it is not what it was, the Holy Trinity Cathedral, built in 1866 to the Gothic design of that most celebrated of Victorian English architects, Sir George Gilbert Scott, still stands on Jiujiang Road. The onion dome of the Russian Orthodox Church on Xinle Road still dominates the city skyline. Nor are these places of worship the only tokens of the Christian faith. To this day beliefs persist: the American Community Church on Hengshan Road (the Avenue Pétain of old) has resumed its services (every Sunday at 7.30 and 10.30 am), and Mass is now sung in the Cathedral of St Ignatius in Xujiahui (Zikawei). The congregations are living survivals of the work of early missionaries. The evangelical tradition was strong in Shanghai where, as in so many other outposts of Western imperialism, the trader, the preacher and the consular official formed the nucleus of the earliest settlement.

Of the monuments to the early missionaries, the Jesuit

Russian Orthodox Church

Cathedral of St Ignatius, Xujiahui

Community Church

Spire being restored to Cathedral of St Ignatius

settlement in Xujiahui is the most impressive. It sprang up in 1847, around the burial mound of Paul Xu Guangqi, who was Matteo Ricci's assistant and Shanghai's first Jesuit convert. There were seminaries where pale-faced young Chinese students conversed in Latin and grappled with knotty theological questions, and convents where local girls sat upon hard seats and worked with eyes screwed up at their lace and embroidery. There was a library housing 200,000 volumes, including the entire run of the Shanghai newspaper *Shen Bao*, local gazetteers from all over the country, and dictionaries and encyclopaedias from all over the world. Presiding over the settlement was the cathedral, a magisterial pile of red brick whose twin spires, hacked away one night by irreverent Red Guards during the Cultural Revolution, have now been restored to it.

The Jesuits were as much scholars as missionaries, and Xujiahui stands more importantly for science than it ever did for religion. Their learned studies of Chinese civilization set

Paul Xu Guangqi

the tone of French sinology, and their manuals acquainted generations of European students with the fundamentals of the Chinese language. It is altogether appropriate that one of the buildings in the cluster is nowadays a branch of the Shanghai Institute of Foreign Languages.

The Catholic fathers were also meteorologists of world repute. The Xujiahui Observatory, a centre of typhoon forecasting built in 1872, was for decades in daily communication with astronomical and meteorological observations throughout the world. It is a lasting memorial, too, to the nineteenth-century belief that spiritual enlightenment through Western science was a very proper aim of Christian endeavour. Today there is life in the old observatory still; for all its creaking old timbers and crumbling brick walls, the building still houses, incredibly, the Shanghai Municipal Meteorological Department.

There are missionary echoes behind Zhongshan Park to the west, part of the old Jessfield Park, a big oblong patch of green on the edges of the city, where the municipal band could be heard to strike up of an evening of a summer's day. It was ordered and spacious, and enclosed a zoo to the west, the St John's University campus in the upper centre, and a loop of the Suzhou Creek to the north. According to placards posted at the entrance, the former university is now the East China Institute of Politics and Law, the Shanghai School of Hygiene and the Graduate Cadres Institute of Health. But the old lecture halls and dormitories gaze down vacantly upon the tree-shaded approaches, and the campus on a dull afternoon during a winter vacation has the solitariness of tombs.

The first cornerstone of St John's was laid by the founders, the American Episcopal Church, in April 1879. The first students, all male, arrived in the following September. Seven girl students were admitted in 1936, and hundreds more enrolled as the years went by. From the first St John's set the pattern for China's Christian colleges. When it

St John's University campus

introduced English courses in 1881, the rest of China caught on and Anglo-Chinese colleges began springing up everywhere. The pages of *Who's Who in China* were studded with the names of its alumni. It was to the adroit steersmanship of F.L. Hawks Pott, its head for fifty-two years, that St John's owed its prestige. He was a dab hand at raising money in America, and it was said that he never made a trip to the United States without returning with a building for the campus tucked into his pocket.

The students were well-heeled and sometimes thought too westernized by half for old-school taste. They were a whole new breed of Chinese, for whom the trappings of Western lifestyle beckoned more seductively than their own. But though many were indeed rich boys and dandies, and spent more time at the Shanghai Stock Exchange than in the classrooms, still the students were like students anywhere — idealistic often, left-leaning sometimes. They could be as defiant as any in the face of authority, as John Dewey found when he visited the university in 1919. It was the Day of Humiliation, a holiday marking the anniversary of the notorious Twenty-One Demands, presented by Japan to the Chinese government in 1915. Japan had entered the world war on the side of the allies and, under the pretext of campaigns against the German holdings in Shandong Province, had driven her imperial stakes deep into northern China. The demands were audacious, and called for nothing less than a China in thrall to an imperious Japan. The nation's moment of shame long rankled in the memory, and here is how, according to John Dewey, the students of St John's remembered it:

"Students walked to Shanghai, ten miles, on the hottest day to parade, then ten miles back. Some of them fell by the way with sunstroke. On their return in the evening they found some of the younger students going in to a concert .... These students stood outside of the door where the concert was to be held and their principal came out and told them they must go to the concert. They replied that they were praying there, as it was not a time for celebrating by a concert on the Day of Humiliation. Then they were ordered to go in first by this principal and afterwards by the President of the whole college. Considerable excitement was the result. Students said they were watching there for the sake of China as the apostles prayed at the death of Christ and this anniversary was like the anniversary of the death of Christ. The President told them if they did not go in then he would shut them out of the college. This he did. They stood there till morning and then one of them who lived nearby took them into his house. Therefore St John's College is closed and the President has not given in."

A Sense of Old Shanghai

How often, on a quest for a past, the imagination conjures up historical relics, buildings with curling roofs, old bridges and arches, only to find, on catching up with the present, that the places have become parking lots, modern housing estates or filling stations. There is little danger of that kind of frustration in Shanghai. It is nearly all there still: bits of London and Paris, a Gothic spire here, a bulbous dome there. Signs of ageing are everywhere: peeling plaster, crumbling stonework, faded lettering, fly-blown awnings that look as though they have not been touched since they were first put up, the grime so old upon them that it must be ingrained into the fabric.

But the relics of old Shanghai are not all material. Its presence lies not only in the eye of the beholder; it echoes in your ears and hangs about your nostrils. To find old Shanghai in the present, we must also think of it as an experience which has been passed down in audible, edible and artistic terms, in images and clichés, strong points and vulnerabilities. A sense of old Shanghai comes by several avenues of perception at once.

Nothing gives you a sharper sense of unbroken continuity than the burst of a Shanghainese tirade upon your ear. Surviving official attempts at language standardization, the Shanghai dialect is raucously alive still. Though *putonghua* (the common language based on Peking speech) has replaced it in all the schools, everywhere in the city you will hear the hiss of the dialect's innumerable sibilants. Nor have the slangy expressions thrown up by the preoccupations of the old society — gambling, whoring, European-bashing and ripping people off — been totally blotted out by having to honour the values of a socialist and straitlaced society.

While the world shifted all around them the Shanghainese clung to the pleasures of the table, however austere their lives may have become in other respects. Shanghai and the exquisitely tasty crabs of the Yangcheng lake have always gone together; for thousands of Shanghai expatriates abroad the very mention of the name is enough to intensify their nostalgia. The two things go together still. Another passion is for hilsa herrings, a river fish found only in the southern waters, and whose special quality, as every Shanghainese knows, lies in its soft scales, far and away the most succulent part of the fish. No changes in political system can ever wean the natives from the old addiction. The traditional specialities flourish still, none more vigorously than the sweet stuffed glutinous rice dumpling from Ningbo, which nowhere in the world is eaten in such large quantities and with so much relish. The homesick Shanghainese from abroad, who fondly remembers all the snacks that one used to be able to buy from the stalls around the Temple of the City God, can go down there today and find the spiced beans, the Nanxiang steamed buns, the fermented glutinous rice soup that he, and his father and grandfather before him, had tucked into with relish.

The reputations of the old restaurants die hard, even if the convulsions of the Cultural Revolution had effaced their names, and replaced them with drearier ones. The names have now been revived, resonant with all the old kudos of their kitchens. Xinya (Sunya), the celebrated Cantonese restaurant on Nanking Road East, still packs 690 people into its three spacious floors. The Xinghua Lou (Apricot Blossom Restaurant) carries on from its 120 years in Fuzhou Road.

The most authentic Shanghai cuisine is still to be found on Fuyou Road, not far from the Yu Yuan; called the Rongshun when it first opened, in the nineteenth century, this eating-house has been around for so long, and is so familiar to the citizenry, that for generations it has been known simply as the Old Restaurant.

European culinary traditions persist too, the menus in many restaurants suggestively French, or German, or Hungarian, even if the dishes themselves are not. Laodachang, whose name has been associated for over half a century with French pastry, still sells meringues and macaroons on Huaihai Road, the Avenue Joffre of yesterday. And about the cream cakes of Xilailin on Nanking Road West, there still hangs the decades-old reputation of Kiesling and Bader's tearoom, which once upon a time Xilailin was. Every Shanghainese chef worth his salt knows the recipe for borsch, that most tenacious of European legacies, now so much a part of Shanghai cuisine that in restaurants from Hongkong to San Francisco, the menus bill it among the *Chinese* soups. The accumulated experience that Shanghai has had of things European has managed to ride out the years of isolation and official inhospitality, and though it is considerably diluted, as it is bound to be, yet it surfaces here and there, and reminds one sharply of old times.

To catch the texture of old Shanghai in all its threads, one must also see how its tissue has been worked into popular imagery and art. Old Shanghai has both inspired, and served as the backdrop for, many works of fiction. Among European works evoking the faded era are *Hotel Schanghai* (1939) by Vicki Baum; *Shanghai Honeymoon* (1946) by Maurice Dekobra; *La Condition Humaine* (1933) by André

Malraux; *The Shanghai Bund Murders* (1933) by Van Wyck Mason and *Erwin in Schanghai* (1934) by Wilhelm Komakichi Nohara; there are dozens more.

In Chinese writing the author who best catches the feel of old Shanghai is Chang Ai-ling. No author is more indigenous to the place. Technically she is Shanghainese: she was born there. Emotionally she is Shanghainese: "I do like the people of Shanghai," she once wrote. Culturally she is cosmopolitan in a way that only the natives of that city could be — authentically, gaining other identities without debasing one's own. Of course all kinds of influences are just as necessary, ecologically, to make writing possible. But in Chang Ai-ling the books come to a large extent out of her experience of Shanghai. In every reader who has been touched by the same experience there will spring that sharp sense of recognition on reading her 1940s stories, so intensely evocative are they of certain Shanghai locutions and habits of mind.

She knows her way about cultivated society, yet successfully conveys the streaks of coarseness that lace its social relations. Sophistication with a touch of vulgarity was of course very much the Shanghai way. Her writing itself bears no mark of provinciality, but in its subject matter it never fights shy of what is conventionally regarded as common. Her own tastes run to the spontaneous and the ordinary. She likes din almost for its own sake ("I am Chinese."), and Shanghai flower-drum opera (the least affected, she finds, of all the forms of Chinese folk music) — for the feel of ordinary life about it, the raucousness and the helter-skelter. Never mind that it had a bad reputation, was considered smutty and fit only for petty-bourgeois ears.

In her fiction the social manners of the Shanghai moneyed class and petty bourgeoisie live on. Asked if she could write about the proletariat, she said no, unless it were about household domestics. Yet it is not necessarily the glamorous side of middle-class life that she depicts: "How gorgeous and brilliant was the European image of Shanghai," she once said to a critic, so unlike the Shanghai she wrote about, which was dismal and sleazy, a society on the wane. Even that society, she went on to add, had disappeared, like Atlantis forever sunk in the sea. It survives, though, in her fiction.

Like the Orient Express and Casablanca, Shanghai has provided many images for the screen, some authentic, others merely clichés. "It too-oo-k more than one man to change my name to Shanghai Lily," drawled Marlene Dietrich in *Shanghai Express,* such a smash hit in 1932 that audiences knew that line by heart across the whole of America. (In Shanghai itself the film created a furore. Its portrayal of Chinese bandit revolutionaries stung national pride, and on opening night, the famous Chinese actor and director Hong Shen leapt onto the stage to stop it in mid-run, a dramatic protest followed by a student demonstration outside the cinema. The director Josef von Sternberg was told that if he ever appeared in China, he would be arrested and punished.) In *The Shanghai Gesture,* all the familiar motifs and

Scene from Shanghai Express

type-figures are woven into the fake but ravishing Oriental imagery: gambling den, women in slinky brocade, an Eurasian voluptuary in tuxedo and fez, Mother Gin-Sling in lacquered black wigs. When Gene Tierney, as Poppy the half-caste, delivers the line "It has a ghastly familiarity, like a half-forgotten dream. Anything could happen here," she may just as easily have been speaking of old Shanghai.

In the Chinese cinema, Shanghai lane life came across vividly in classics like *Crows and Sparrows* and *Street Angel*, the latter's opening shot, a long camera movement from the roofs of the city's skyscrapers to the banks of a mucky canal vividly summing up Shanghai. Shanghai was the begetter of the Chinese film industry and its own biggest market. Here the cinema whipped up so much popular enthusiasm that it sometimes bordered on fever. Although the film *Song of the Fisherman* was released at the height of the worst heat wave Shanghai had experienced in sixty years, in June 1934, it ran for 84 days, while the temperature soared to 104 degrees and

Ruan Lingyu

sweat drenched the bodies of the audience.

Today every Chinese over fifty knows the names of movie queens like the great Miss Butterfly Wu (Hu Die) and the delectable Ruan Lingyu, whose own brief off-screen life reads like a film script. Born in Shanghai in 1910, she committed suicide when she was barely 24. Her death galvanized the nation, and it is said that on the day of her funeral, three women killed themselves, their suicide note reading: "If Ruan Lingyu is dead, what else is there to live for?" The *New York Times* correspondent in Shanghai filed a report illustrated by a cartoon showing among the funeral procession a man dressed in a dragon robe and with a white band wound round his head. Everyone knew what it meant: on this day, even the emperor, had there still been one left in China, would come to mourn. Her memory lingers still; perhaps none is more haunted by it than Jiang Qing, who invokes her in her conversations with her American biographer, and who, unlike Ruan Lingyu, did not make it in Shanghai showbiz.

Another enduring figure of legend is Zhou Xuan, the "golden-throated" star of the 1930s and 1940s. Also a creature of tragedy, she died before she was thirty-eight, broken by heartless men. She became quite mad in her last years, her emotional suffering so great that it had to be turned into illness.

What else survives? Of habits of speech and tastes there are many lingering traces. In temper too, there are vestiges from the past. The Shanghainese will always be the first to plump for consumerism. In the old days nothing was more Shanghainese than an excessive open-handedness, a tendency to splurge, often vulgarized in showiness and swagger. The parvenu insisted on paying every bill, and would play the host even at parties given by somebody else. All this was summed up in the epithet *haipai* — a term originally applied to the Shanghai style of opera, but which all detractors use in its alternative interpretation, the Shanghai way of life. *Haipai*

Zhou Xuan

is of course incompatible with the prevailing ideology, but you only need to lower the barricades a little to find it not altogether suppressed.

Shanghai's vocation has not been government, or art or religion; it has been money-making. It has never been mandarin; its idol was mammon and its heart lay wholly in the marketplace. It has produced no great statesman or claimant to the dragon throne, but it has never been short of businessmen, and the talents of its industrialists, bankers, shippers, publishers and wheeler-dealers linger noticeably on. Take any trade delegation from China, and see if the most wily members aren't from Shanghai.

Chang Ai-ling once wrote that the Shanghainese was a traditional Chinese tempered by the high tension of modern life, the quirky and perhaps not too healthy offspring of the mingling of cultures old and new. It is a mixture out of which has come a curious intelligence. If he is wicked, Chang Ai-ling says, his wickedness is never without a sense of proportion. He may be a ruthless opportunist and a great one for fishing in troubled waters, yet because he knows his way around the world he knows precisely just how far to go. She uses the Chinese word *tong* to describe the Shanghai native — a word implying savvy, grasp, a comprehensiveness of mind. It summarises at once the good and the bad of Shanghainese mentality: the good — a certain *savoir-faire*, an intelligence, a know-how which made Shanghai the most switched-on of cities; the bad — a know-all complacency, an unwillingness to hear another out, a tendency to sharp practice and a conviction that the skills, crafts and expertise of all China radiate outwards from downtown Shanghai.

The old skills have not died out, and for Chinese all over the country, "Made in Shanghai" is still the mark and guarantee of quality. No matter what it is that you want to buy, whether it is a bicycle or a watch, a sweater or a television set, it is best to get one that is made in Shanghai. Even Jiang Qing had her wig made here, at the Yong Qing (Forever Young) hairpiece shop near Chenghuang Miao. To the world outside Shanghai is backward and outmoded, but for the rest of China it still sets the style. No swanky socialite sweeps into the hotel foyers, but go to a dinner party at one of the top restaurants, and see if you can't feel the polish of an earlier age perpetuated, a sense of worldly style preserved. In the end this is bound to change, as the old sophistication recedes and new tastes emerge, all ill-digested modernity and crude imitation. But the time is not yet. The transition will pass many people by, and in them old Shanghai will endure, like the tough survivor it always was.

A Note on Sources

Much of the material for this book was picked up on a trip which the photographer, Antonio Hin Yeung Mak, and I made to Shanghai in February 1981. I also consulted an older generation's memories and a wide range of published sources. The literature on Shanghai is very large and I name here only those works from which I have directly quoted or taken illustrations, or which I have repeatedly consulted.

The quotations in the book (in the order in which they appear) were from *The Capital of the Tycoon* by Rutherford Alcock (London, 1863); *Hudson Taylor in Early Years* by Howard Taylor (London, 1932); *Trade and Diplomacy on the China Coast* by John F. Fairbank (Cambridge, Mass., 1953); *Present Indicative* by Noel Coward (London, 1937); *The Sassoons* by Stanley Jackson (London, 1968); *Foreign Devils in the Flowery Kingdom* by Carl Crow (London, 1941); *Fun in a Chinese Laundry* by Josef von Sternberg and *The May Fourth Movement* by Chow Tse-tsung (Stanford, 1960).

My translation of the May Fourth Movement jingle was based on a quotation of the original in *Wu-Si aiguo yundong*, volume II (Peking, 1979). My translation of the passage from the novel *Qiu Haitang* was based on the excerpt quoted in *Yuanyang-Hudie-pai yanjiu zhiliao* edited by Wei Shaochang (Shanghai, 1962).

I could not have written the book without *Shanghai-tong* (Shanghai, 1936); *Shanghai chunqiu* (Hong Kong, 1968) and

Shanghai zhinan (Shanghai, 1980). Also useful were *Jiu Shanghai de gushi* (Shanghai, 1963); *Shanghai Waitan Nanjing Lu de shihua* (Shanghai, 1976); *Shanghai geming yiji de gushi* (Shanghai, 1978); *Shanghai xianhua* (Tapiei, 1961) and *Gudao jianwen* (Shanghai, 1979).

The sources of the illustrations are listed below. Pictures not included in the list were taken by Antonio Hin Yeung Mak for the book.

The British Film Institute: 131

Da Zangjing, edited by Huang Zongyang(Shanghai,1909): 74

Dianshi Zhai Huabao (Shanghai, 1893-96), used by permission of the British Library: 11, 17, 53, 55, 68

The Essex Institute, Salem, Massachusetts: 29

Historic Shanghai by C.A. Montalto de Jesus (Shanghai, 1909): 39, 123

The Hongkong & Shanghai Bank archives: 15, 16

Jim Hornabrook: Sassoon villa (colour)

Jiangshan duo jiao (Shanghai, 1979): 9

Joint Publishing Company (Hongkong): Tomb of Lu Xun, A view of Shanghai (colour)

Li Wei-i: 94, 120, (top), 121

M. Miller: 110

C. M. Pan: 56

Rou Shi xuanji (Peking, 1958): 113

Shanghai de guanghui geming shiji tuji, compiled by the Committee for the Preservation of the Historical Relics of Shanghai (Shanghai, 1978): 63, 65, 81, 102, 107

Shanghai Saga by John Pal (London, 1963): 96

Shanghai of Today, compiled by the North China Daily News (Shanghai, 1928): 72

The Soong Sisters by Emily Hahn (London, 1942): 48

Twentieth Century Impressions of Shanghai, edited by Arnold Wright and H.A. Cartwright (London, 1908): 66

Zhongguo yintan waishi (Hongkong, 1976): 132

Index

About the Author

Pan Ling, who now lives in London, was born in Shanghai, spent much of her childhood in North Borneo, and worked in Geneva, Helsinki and Hong Kong. Her first book was on international drug legislation. Her writing has since broadened to include subjects related to China. She has just completed a book on psychoactive drugs and a narrative history revolving around the figure of Du Yuesheng, old Shanghai's city boss.

《上海掌故》　潘　翎著

三聯書店（香港）有限公司出版

香港中環域多利皇后街九號